Kids Who Mak

K I D S
WHO MAKE A
DIFFERENCE

Joyce M. Roche,

Marie Rodriguez,

& Phyllis Schneider

MASTERMEDIA LIMITED · NEW YORK

MASTERMEDIA and colophon are registered trademarks
of MasterMedia Limited.

LOC Cataloging-in-Publication data

Roche, Joyce M.
Kids who make a difference / Joyce M. Roche. Maria Rodriguez, and
Phyllis Schneider.
p. cm.
Summary: Describes ways in which children have helped their
communitits and the world by working on such problems as the
environment, drugs, and health care.
ISBN 0-942361-59-8
1. Children as volunteers—United States—Juvenile literature.
2. Social action—United States—Juvenile literature.
[1. Volunterism.] I. Rodriguez, Marie. II. Schneider, Phyllis.
III. Title.
HO784.V64R83   1993
305.23—dc20   92-35583
CIP
AC

Designed by Jacqueline Schuman
Production services by Martin Cook Associates, New York, NY
Manufactured in the United States of America

Contents

Contents

Preface: To Teachers and Parents

We hope this book will stimulate discussion between parent or teacher and child and nurture children's self-esteem.

The following advice was suggested by Anne Fletcher, a teacher who is also the head of a division of lower schools:

Before you read, select a chapter and ask your children to express what they know already about the general topic (drugs, alcohol, manatees, libraries). This brief discussion will increase comprehension of the story being read silently or aloud.

After the reading, ask your group of listeners to comment on what was surprising to them about the section. You might say, "Were you surprised by anything you learned from this story?"

Try not to direct the child's thinking too much. Allowing children to respond spontaneously will encourage thinking practice and make it an active process. The children will tell you what they are thinking about and what the story means to them. You might end the discussion by asking, "Why do you suppose the authors wanted you to read about this person?"

Acknowledgments

The authors wish to thank the following people and organizations for their invaluable contributions to this book: Ann Medlock, and the entire staff of the Giraffe Project; the Carnegie Hero Fund Commission; Ellen Anderson, and the Clairol Spirit of Young America Awards; Big Brothers/Big Sisters of America; Deborah Purcell; Laura Grill, of the Harrison, N.Y., Public Library.

Kids Who Make a Difference

Introduction: A Call to Action!

Hunger, homelessness, poverty. Global warming, the destruction of our rain forests and the ozone layer. AIDS, cancer, birth defects. The killing of endangered species, and millions of unwanted, homeless pets. Drug and alcohol addiction, drunk driving, racism, violence in our streets—and schools.

Sometimes, the problems our world faces seem overwhelming—and it's tempting to wonder if we can solve those problems, if our individual efforts can make a difference. Is *trying* to help really worth it?

Fifteen-year-old Ellen Bigger, of Key Largo, Florida, is convinced that the actions of even *one* person—and kids in particular—can, and will, make our world a better, safer place. Ellen lost two people she cared deeply about to drug-related deaths, and when she was five, she and several other kindergarten kids were caught in the cross fire between a police SWAT team and a drugged-out sniper. Many of the adults in Ellen's community had become cynical; they felt there was nothing they could do to stop the dealers, who actually knocked on people's front doors to sell drugs!

But Ellen believed that kids have power, that a kid *can* get other young people *and* adults to listen—and make a difference. She founded an organization called "Drug-Free Homes" and launched an all-out war on drugs in her community. Ellen Bigger is just one of the many remarkable kids we'll introduce you to in this book.

Throughout history, young people have made a difference through their determination, idealism, innovative ideas, and actions. And some have even shaped world events.

In 1830, 12-year-old Frederick Douglass, a black slave living in Baltimore, Maryland, overheard his masters say that slaves shouldn't be allowed to learn how to read or write—because that knowledge could help them devise ways to escape. Frederick became *determined* to learn and convinced several white children to teach him. Armed with his ability to read, he studied speeches in the *Columbia Orator* and learned as much as he could about rights and liberty issues. When Frederick was 20, he escaped, traveled to New York, and became one of the most powerful forces in the antislavery movement. He continued his fight for "equality for all" until his death at age 77, encouraging both blacks *and* women to strive for equal rights.

Blinded in an accident when he was three, Louis Braille, of Coupvray, France, attended a special school where he longed to read like other children. Hoping to develop a "code" or system that would allow *all* blind kids and adults to read books and newspapers, 11-year-old Louis spent long hours trying to create "letters" the blind could feel with their fingertips. After several years of unsuccessful work on his project, Louis was about to give up—then he met a French army captain, Charles Barbier, who had invented a system for sending messages in the dark. Called "night writing," Barbier's code consisted of raised dots and dashes on pieces of paper; by touching the raised dots and dashes, soldiers could translate messages without having to use a torch. By 1824, Louis, 15, had created a writing and reading technique based on dots and dashes—the Braille system—that has allowed millions of blind people worldwide to read.

There are dozens—even hundreds—of other amazing kids who've left their mark on history. Young people like 16-year-old Sacajawea, a Shoshone Indian girl, who, in 1804, acted as an interpreter for the famed Lewis and Clark expedition. And Anne Frank, the courageous Jewish-German teen who, with her family, spent almost three years hiding in an unused area of an office building in Amsterdam, hoping to escape the Nazis, who were committed to killing every Jew on the Continent during World War II. Anne died in a German concentration camp at Belsen in 1945. But she left behind a beautiful and moving record of her family's life in seclusion—*The Diary of a Young Girl.* In it, Anne said she wanted to go on living, even after her death, and her diary has inspired millions of people.

These outstanding young people have their counterparts today, in our world, in our time, in our own neighborhoods. People like Edward Huynh, a student at the University of California-Davis, who fled from Vietnam to the United States in 1985, when he was 17. (Edward and his family had been jailed in Vietnam after the overthrow of Saigon; eventually, they were among the thousands of "boat people" who escaped.) Edward couldn't speak English when he first came to America, but he learned how to speak the language—and to read and write it—and he's spent many hours as a hospital volunteer in Sacramento, reading fairy tales to young emergency room patients "to comfort them."

People like Patrick Long, 20, of Bellevue, Washington, who fought—and won—his battle with leukemia during his early teen years, and has committed his life to counseling *other* young cancer patients.

Kids like 16-year-old Aja Henderson, of Baton Rouge, Louisiana, who created a 3,000-book library in her home "for kids who aren't able to get to a regular library, but need a place to study or to develop a lifelong love of reading."

Courageous kids like 13-year-old Joey DiPaolo, of Brooklyn,

New York, who contracted AIDS from a blood transfusion when he was four—and has spent the last few years working to educate children and adults about the HIV virus, and AIDS-related issues.

All, in large—or small—ways, are heroes who've given up much of their free time to help others. We hope their stories will inspire you to do the same (to help you get started, we've included suggestions, and names and addresses of volunteer organizations at the end of each story, as well as in the Resources section at the end of the book).

Thirty-two years ago—long before any of the kids you'll meet in this book were born!—President John F. Kennedy challenged Americans to prove themselves with his famous inaugural declaration, "Ask *not* what your country can do for you. Ask what *you* can do for your country!" Today, our challenge is even greater: What can *you* do to make your nation, our world, a better, safer, more peaceful place for everyone? The challenge is yours—because, as a young person, you *are* the future.

Fighting for a Better, Safer World, Supporting "Kids' Rights"

Ellen Bigger

Andrea Eaton

Margaret Ann Sisler

Teddy Andrews

Robert Cobbley

Marcey Perry

Aja Henderson

Joshua Raiford

Linda Warsaw

Jennifer Sussal

Winning the War on Drugs

ELLEN BIGGER

Ellen Bigger mounted her own personal war on drugs in part because of drug-related tragedies that affected her life.

"The day I was born, a very close relative, who was on drugs and alcohol, committed suicide," says the 15-year-old Key Largo, Florida, girl. When Ellen was five, she and a group of other kindergarten kids were caught in the cross fire between a police SWAT team and a sniper who was high on drugs. "And when I was 10, my Girl Scout leader was killed by someone on drugs," she says.

Then, four years ago, Ellen and her Scout troop attended the commissioning ceremony of the Coast Guard cutter *Key Largo*. "The captain talked about the importance of fighting the drug problem and the need for civilians (both adults and kids) to help. [Part of the Coast Guard's mission is to keep drugs from being smuggled into this country.] His speech and his own dedication made me want to do something to help," says Ellen.

Her answer to the captain's challenge was to start a program called "Drug-Free Homes." "A lot of adults in the community had become very cynical about the drug problem," she explains. "Where I live in South Florida, drugs are everywhere and many adults felt overwhelmed; they believed nothing could be done. So I printed up brochures that explained why I was starting Drug-Free Homes, telling about the dangers of drugs, etc. On the back was a pledge form everyone in the house was required to sign. Once they signed, I sent them a sticker for their door or window, reading, 'This Is a Drug-Free Home. Every Member Within Has Signed a Pledge to Live a Drug-Free Life.' When the dealers see the stickers, they don't come to those houses. The sticker is also an emblem of pride—it shows that the whole family is proud of being drug-free. And if people in the community see that even one family has a sticker up, they have the courage to sign the pledge too and post a sticker on *their* homes."

Although United Way and the Girl Scout Council of Tropical Florida footed a major part of the bill for printing the first batch of brochures and stickers, Drug-Free Homes is basically self-supporting, according to Ellen. "I raise money by selling T-shirts and buttons with the insignia, 'I live in a drug-free home and I'm proud of it.' "

Ellen distributes the Drug-Free Homes brochures to neighbors and to schoolchildren. She travels regularly in Florida (and sometimes to other states), making speeches at elementary and junior high schools. "Most of the kids I talk to are in grade school," she notes. "This is a drug *prevention* program; I try to get to the kids when they're young, *before* they've made the decision to do drugs. I give them important information that will help them make the right decision."

Because of her one-person crusade against drugs, Ellen was honored by the Giraffe Project (an organization that recognizes people who "stick their necks out for others") and was invited to tour the Soviet Union with other "Giraffes" two summers

Ellen Bigger.

ago. "We talked with young Soviets about possible solutions for world peace and other concerns their country shared with ours." While on tour, Ellen formed close friendships with several of the American Giraffes and was excited by the volunteer projects *they* were involved in—everything from counseling children with cancer to spearheading environmental causes.

"Talking with them made me realize there was so much more I wanted to get involved in besides drug prevention," says Ellen. "But there are so many possible areas for volunteerism—I couldn't do *everything* I wanted to. So I decided to start an organization called Youthwish, which helps other kids who have ideas for volunteer projects get started."

As head of Youthwish (now an international organization), Ellen receives letters from kids around the world asking for her advice on everything from working with the homeless to starting an antiviolence program at school. "Most kids say, 'I want to do such-and-such, but I don't know how to get started,'" Ellen explains. "I give the best advice I can; if I'm not able to supply advice about a particular area, I find out who *can* help. For example, one girl wanted to start a program to combat violence in her school (kids were getting stabbed and shot). I contacted the Giraffe Project, and they sent me a list of kids who'd started similar programs."

Ellen says the hardest part about juggling her two nonprofit organizations with the demands of school is that "often, I've been away on speaking engagements, and when I get home my schoolwork has really piled up. That's when I ask myself, 'Why do I bother?' I've asked other Giraffes if they've ever felt like quitting, and they say they do, too. But we keep going because we're trying to make a difference. Sometimes, I don't know how much of an impact I've made until a year after I've spoken at a particular school about the drug problem, and a mother comes up and tells me how excited *her* child was about my speech, and how he's said, 'I'll *never* do drugs!' I tell someone about the dangers of doing drugs, and they tell their friends. There's a ripple effect. And I may be influencing a particular kid to want to do something similar to Drug-Free Homes when he or she is a little older."

Would you like to start a Drug-Free Homes program in your area? Or do you have questions about other types of volunteer projects? Write to Youthwish, Inc., 27 Eagle Drive, Key Largo, FL 33037. Enclose a self-addressed, stamped, legal-size envelope.

Stopping Teen Suicides

ANDREA EATON

W hen her Bozeman, Montana, high school was rocked by three suicides, Andrea Eaton knew she had to do something. "We hadn't had a death in our school system since 1987, and that was the result of an accident," says Andrea. "Having three kids commit suicide—all within a year [a *fourth* suicide occurred the following year]—was very hard to deal with. Nobody in the school or community seemed to be confronting the issue.

"I wanted to get people together to talk about suicide, to recognize the warning signs [in their friends, or children], to figure out *why* kids take their lives, and what can be done to prevent this from happening."

In 1990, Andrea attended a national conference on teen suicide, sponsored by Camp Fire. Then, with the help of a school guidance counselor, she formed a support group consisting of eight students. "We talked about our feelings regarding the deaths," Andrea explains, "as well as how parental expectations, family problems, peer pressure and [the availability of] drugs and alcohol can all put a great deal of stress on kids.

Andrea Eaton.

"We also discussed how the importance our community places on having money and a lot of nice clothes and other material things makes some kids (who *don't* have such luxuries) feel left out and hopeless."

The group met weekly for 50-minute sessions and focused on a variety of activities and issues, including relaxation exercises, stress-reduction techniques, goal-setting skills, and ways to build self-esteem ("A lack of self-esteem seems to play a part in teen suicide," explains Andrea).

Eager to make *adults* in the community more aware of the teen-suicide problem, Andrea joined a local suicide-prevention group called LIFE (Living Is For Everyone), becoming the only teen member on the governing board. LIFE then joined forces with another group, the Prevention Coalition, and together the organizations met with the Bozeman superintendent of schools to discuss ways to prevent suicide within the system. The groups also held seminars on suicide prevention, sponsored community meetings, and handed out pamphlets explaining how to determine whether a teen is at risk.

Now 19 and a freshman at Montana State University, Andrea is continuing her involvement in suicide prevention and plans to join the Task Force, a team of firefighters, police officers, counselors, psychiatrists, and concerned community residents. "This group actually goes out and intervenes *before* a teen can attempt suicide," she explains.

Andrea, who was a 1991 recipient of the Clairol Spirit of Young America Award, also hopes to become a teacher and plans to use her knowledge of suicide prevention when working with young kids. "I've been involved in Camp Fire for many years," she says, noting that she's regularly served as a camp counselor. "At camp, I try to work with kids to help them develop self-esteem. If I become a teacher, I'd like to incorporate a 'self-esteem-building' program into the curriculum (and, perhaps, into an entire school system's curriculum). I believe that a lack of self-esteem leads to many problems kids face, as well as playing a major role in suicide. If I can get to kids early, when they're young, and help them feel good about themselves, I may play a part in preventing serious problems from surfacing later on."

Would you like to start a suicide-prevention, peer-counseling, or support group at your school? Talk with the school guidance counselor, who can help you form a group, as well as put you in touch with local suicide-prevention organizations.

Also, consider volunteering to work on a crisis-intervention hotline, talking with upset or lonely kids who are contemplating suicide. To locate an area hotline, check the "Community Services" section in your telephone book (usually located at the front of the book).

For more info on suicide prevention, contact the Youth Suicide National Center at 415-342-5755.

To become involved in Camp Fire, contact your area branch, or write or call the national headquarters at: 4601 Madison Avenue, Kansas City, MO 64112-1278; 816-756-1950.

A Pair of Helping Hands

MARGARET ANN SISLER

Margaret Ann Sisler, 12, lent not one, but two, helping hands when she took part in her school's sixth grade/first grade "buddy" program last year.

For nine months, Margaret Ann, of Bruceton Mills, West Virginia, spent a half hour each morning with Clint, a seven-year-old who has Down syndrome. (Clint, now a second-grader, was mainstreamed into public school and attends classes with nonhandicapped children.)

In order to communicate with Clint, Margaret Ann learned English sign language. "I learned it during recesses," she says. "Mrs. Suzanne Viski, the speech teacher at our school, taught me." Margaret Ann adds that although Clint *is* able to speak, he has some trouble sounding out words, so he communicates by using a combination of sign language *and* speech.

During their sessions with Clint, Margaret Ann and Mrs. Viski helped the boy learn how to communicate more easily with other students. But, first, he had to develop a feeling of trust. "He wouldn't talk to me at all when I started working with him," recalls Margaret Ann. "Finally, he began to talk and sign

Margaret Ann, with buddy Clint McKinney.

to me. From then on, he learned quickly and followed instructions well. For example, if we asked him to get a cup of water to water the plants, he'd do it right away.

"He also became much more outgoing with the other kids and talked more with them [Margaret Ann and Mrs. Viski taught Clint to use a mix of both sign and verbal language the other kids could understand]. Now, when someone walking down the hall says 'Hi' to him, he says 'Hi' right back!"

Margaret Ann, who'd like to become a psychologist working with both adults *and* kids, says Clint is a very good student. "He didn't get frustrated or upset when he didn't understand something, or couldn't say something the right way," she notes. "He kept on trying. He just wants to be like everyone else."

What was the best part about being a buddy to Clint? "I think it was really neat to get to work with him," says Margaret Ann, "because he's such a *nice* person [Clint gave Margaret Ann lots of hugs at the end of their sessions]. And because I learned sign language, I can talk to [hearing-impaired] people too."

Would you like to learn more about Down syndrome? For a free information packet, call or write to the National Down Syndrome Society, 666 Broadway, New York, NY 10012; 1-800-221-4602.

Interested in learning sign language? For info on a training center in your area, write or call the Deafness Research Foundation, 9 East 38th Street, 7th Floor, New York, NY 10016; 1-800-535-3323.

He's Into "Kid Stuff"

TEDDY ANDREWS

Teddy Andrews was only seven when he was appointed to the Berkeley, California, Youth Commission.

"I'd worked on the reelection campaign of a city council member," Teddy, now 11, explains, "and she appointed me to the commission." Soon after, Teddy came up with the idea of a citywide Wish List to help homeless and needy children. He and several volunteers toured homeless shelters and various recreational programs in the area and asked these organizations what they needed most. "We compiled the list, then tried to get the people what they wanted," says Teddy. "The top three needs were paper and pencils (so the kids could do their homework) and books so they could practice reading."

Teddy is also founder of S.A.Y. Y.A.Y.! (Save American Youth/Youth Advocates for Youth), a kid-run organization boasting more than 400 members. "I realized that a lot of children's organizations didn't have any children [on the governing boards]," says Teddy, "so I talked with the executive director of B.O.S.S. [Berkeley-Oakland Support Services], the largest provider in the Bay Area, and told her that this was 'age

Teddy Andrews.

discrimination.' She agreed, and we set up S.A.Y. Y.A.Y.!'"

The organization has sponsored the city's first environmental egg hunt, as well as the first and second annual Christmas toy drives, solicited funds for a municipal Christmas tree, and provided free vaccinations for needy kids.

"When we learned that many homeless children had no place to go, other than doorways, when they were sick, we set up a 24-hour shelter for families with kids," adds Teddy. "We also established a learning center, equipped with computers, paper and pencils, books, and other items. The center is located in a trailer behind Harrison House, one of the B.O.S.S.-sponsored shelters. It's a place where kids can go to learn— *and* socialize with their peers." (A teacher is available to help the children with their homework.)

Teddy says his interest in helping children evolved when he was named to the Youth Commission, but he admits he's always been an advocate for kids. "Adults are old children," Teddy points out. "They should respect children because we are the future. . . . I think that children can make a difference." And Teddy Andrews is living proof!

Want to get involved in *your* city or state government—and make your opinions known? Volunteer to work on a political campaign (city council, gubernatorial [candidates for governor], state and U.S. House and Senate, and presidential candidates all welcome volunteers). Contact your area Republican or Democratic parties for more info.

Also, write to your city council representative and ask if your area has a "youth commission." Find out how you can get involved if one does exist. If your city *doesn't* have a youth commission, volunteer to start one!

On Their Own—But Not "Alone"

ROBERT COBBLEY

Robert Cobbley knows what it's like to "go it alone." He left home at 16 ("because of disagreements with my new stepmother"), stayed at a friend's house for a while, ended up on the streets for several days, and finally rented a "little rundown apartment.

"I'd been working part-time at a fast-food restaurant," says Robert, "so I asked my boss if I could work full-time after school." In order to buy groceries and pay his rent, he took on a *second* job—clerking at a department store.

Robert adds that the stress of supporting himself while attending school was tremendous, and many times he was tempted to drop out. But he realized how important an education was to his future. In order to help *other* kids deal with the pressures of living alone, working full-time, and going to school, the Pocatello, Idaho, boy founded SOTO (Students on Their Own) at his high school.

"I wanted to encourage kids to stay in school when they were tempted to drop out," he explains. "At first, I didn't know if the program would work, but I wrote to school administra-

Robert Cobbley.

tors, telling them what I had in mind. They were very interested and assigned a counselor to work on the project with me."

Besides being a support group for kids, SOTO also provides other valuable services for members (between 14 and 30 kids are involved in SOTO at any given time). Meetings often feature speakers who "talk about everything from health issues to job training. The local Family Planning Advisory Board sent speakers who gave us information on sex education and birth control," says Robert. "After all, we wanted to prevent kids from *having* kids.

"A woman who worked for a local insurance company arranged for special health insurance rates for the students—$19 a month per person. The Southeast Idaho Community Action Agency helped us locate affordable housing, so no one had to stay on the streets. Idaho Power gave us special rates so we could afford heat in our apartments," Robert notes.

The students in SOTO came from various backgrounds. "In some cases, both parents had died and the kid was on his own. Some were runaways. Others had stayed behind when their parents had moved," explains Robert, who adds that the members of the group participated in social activities on a regular basis. "Our counselor got a small state grant for the group, and we were able to pay for lunch for the members once a week. Other times, we all went bowling or to the movies or skating."

Robert, who recently turned 20, joined the marines right after graduating from high school. Today, he's a marine reservist, and plans to start college soon ("I'd like to become a teacher," he says). Robert has also reconciled with his family, and though he's no longer totally "on his own," he remains active in SOTO (which now has a branch in another area high school), occasionally attending meetings and frequently checking with faculty advisers to "keep up to date." He's very proud of the organization—and of its members. "When I went into the marines, three kids went off to college," he notes. "Another went to work for a radio station. Only one student didn't make it through high school—the rest are sticking with it."

To start a group like SOTO in *your* school, propose your idea (in writing) to a guidance counselor, vice principal, or principal. Once you have the school's support, arrange for a regular meeting place (a study hall or classroom), then run an announcement in the school newspaper, or post notices on bulletin boards.

Turning Kids' Lives Around

MARCEY PERRY

Marcell Perry tried to commit suicide when she was in the ninth grade. Today, the 19-year-old Atlanta girl has turned her own personal story of tragedy into one of triumph—and she now helps *other* kids overcome serious problems and take control of *their* lives.

"I was very depressed," says Marcey, adding that she'd been a straight-A student in elementary school, but by ninth grade was on the verge of flunking out. "Overnight, I went from straight A's to D's and F's. Physically, I was in school. Mentally, I was somewhere else." Marcey explains that her emotional problems were sparked by a number of things. "I was trying to deal with being 'in love' for the first time," she says. "I was also having a lot of problems with my mother and we weren't communicating." Marcey was also keeping a secret: for eight months she had been molested by her step-grandfather.

"For a long time, I didn't tell anybody he was molesting me," Marcey admits. "My family is very religious, and I was afraid of hurting them. Finally, I told a cousin, who told my mother. She confronted my grandfather."

But by then Marcey had slipped into a deep depression, and she decided to end her life by taking 10 of her grandmother's sleeping pills. "I ended up in a coma for 24 hours and spent the next two weeks in the hospital," Marcey recalls. The doctors evaluated her emotional condition and recommended that she be admitted to a psychiatric hospital. "I was there for six months, going through therapy and taking a lot of medication, but none of it helped," she says.

Then, Marcey's aunt suggested that her niece enroll in Rich's Academy in Atlanta (Rich's is an "alternative high school," formed in 1981 for dropouts and students at risk of dropping out). Rich's provided the turning point for Marcey. "It's a very unique school in that there are so few students [20 per teacher, versus 40 for every teacher in regular public high school]," says Marcey. "The students get individualized attention, and the teachers don't focus just on academics. They know that if you're having a hard time at home, there's no way you can concentrate on English and math, so they also work with us on the personal aspects of our lives. They help students develop self-esteem and set goals. We each have our teacher's home phone number. Many times, I've had to call my teacher when my mom and I had gotten into an argument, and my teacher helped both of us tremendously."

At Rich's, Marcey was able to work through her depression and turn her energies to helping other people. She joined the Exodus Players, a group of students who tour the country, performing at schools and city centers. "We use music, drama, and poetry [much of it written by the students] to tell kids how we overcame our problems—and how they can overcome theirs," says Marcey. "My presentation deals mostly with being molested. Another girl talks about how her father killed himself. One student tells how he needed an 'attitude adjustment,'

Marcey Perry.

and another tells how she had a lot of problems after her mother died." (Marcey has also traveled with another Rich's group, which focuses on helping kids develop self-esteem.)

The Exodus Players also perform for adults. "We try to teach them to understand what's *really* going on with young people," says Marcey. "We've performed for President Bush, Sidney Poitier, Lee Iacocca [the Chrysler chairman], and at mayors' conferences."

Marcey recently made a trip to New York City to help a pharmaceutical company produce a video about teen sexuality. "One person from every region of the country appears in the video," she explains. "I represent the Southeast. We talk about how young people view sexuality and what's proper and what's not." (The video has been distributed to 9,000 high schools.)

Marcey also served for two years as youth coordinator for the National Youth Action for Change Conference in Atlanta. Held at the World Congress Center, the conference attracted 1,100 teens from around the country. "We had 10 workshops focusing on issues like teen pregnancy, sexuality, drug and alcohol abuse, and leadership development," notes Marcey. "The workshops were all led by young people—because kids listen to their peers."

Today, as Marcey looks back on her life, she's "amazed. Just a few years ago, I was sure I would always be depressed and suicidal. I had my mind made up. Now, I look at all the things I'm doing, the difference I'm able to make in other people's lives. It's made me feel really good about myself.

"After a performance [with the Exodus Players], I've had numerous kids come up to me and say, 'I'm being molested, but I don't know who to tell or *how* to tell it.' One time, after we'd performed at a particular school, the principal called me the next day. She said one of the students who'd seen my presentation had come up to her and said, 'This is happening to me. I'm being molested by my uncle. I need help.' "

When it comes to taking advice—and asking for help—kids turn to other kids. If *you'd* like to help kids who are in trouble (or at risk for drug or alcohol abuse, teen pregnancy, running away, or molestation, for example), volunteer as a crisis-intervention hotline counselor, or work with your school administration to develop a "peer counseling" program.

For more information about how you can help kids turn their lives around, contact these organizations:

National Committee for Prevention of Child Abuse, 312-663-3520; the National Crime Prevention Council, 202-466-6272 (this organization can help you—and your school—start a peer counseling program); National Runaway Switchboard, 312-880-9866; Runaway Hotline, 1-800-231-6946; the American Council for Drug Education, 301-294-0600; Just Say No Clubs, 1-800-258-2766; National Council on Alcoholism, 212-206-6770.

Aja Henderson is into books in a big way. "I've always loved reading," says the 16-year-old from Baton Rouge, Louisiana, so setting up a library in her home seemed a natural thing to do. "There were a lot of children in my community who didn't have anyone to take them to regular libraries," she explains. "Most had parents who both worked, and by the time the parents got home, the libraries were closed."

Aja was just 12 when she opened *her* library (situated in her family's den. "My dad gets thrown out of the den a lot," she admits, "but he doesn't mind"). The teen initially used many of her old books to stock the library, and also accepted donations from people in the neighborhood. "At first, the library was just intended for kids," she says, "but, eventually, grownups started coming, too." Today, Aja's library attracts "everyone from very young children to teens to adults."

With more than 3,000 titles (including cookbooks and reference works), an assortment of magazines, several sets of encyclopedias, and various textbooks, the library "offers something for everyone," says Aja. "I have books that appeal to boys as well as girls, novels, and nonfiction works. If someone comes to the library more than once, I learn that person's name and find out what types of books he likes. Then, I look around for other books that might appeal to him."

Aja added a collection of textbooks "so kids who left their books at school could stop by the library, find the text they needed, then do their homework. That way, they don't fall into the trap of not doing an assignment, then missing another one, and falling so far behind they never catch up."

The library is open seven days a week "and there aren't any set hours. Sometimes people knock on our door early in the morning before I go to school, or someone stops by pretty late at night. I never turn anyone away. I'm proud that people like to read, and that they'd even give up a Saturday afternoon to spend time at my library," she says. Though kids were sometimes teased and called "bookworms" for frequenting Aja's library when it first opened, that doesn't happen anymore. "Now, *everyone* in the neighborhood is a bookworm!" she explains, adding that the community is very proud and supportive of the library.

And although some people are amazed that Aja has been so successful in her venture, she says, "I'm just a normal American kid. If *I* can do something like this, so can other kids. It just takes a little work and some creativity. You don't have to have a lot of money to start a library. Just go around your neighborhood and find out what types of books and magazines people are interested in. If there are a lot of little kids, try to get their parents to donate used books and magazines so *everyone* can enjoy them."

Aja has built her vast collection by frequenting used-book stores ("You can get lots of good books for very little money," she notes). Her appearance on local TV news programs has

Aja Henderson.

also generated donations. And the Library of Congress, as well as the publishing giant Macmillan, has helped stock the library.

Aja *does* give up some of her free time to run the library (her mom takes over when the teen is at school). But Aja adds, "I think it's important to help people, especially children, explore reading and gain an appreciation for literary works. I want them to discover books as an alternative to watching TV or just 'hanging out.' And books offer knowledge; when you have knowledge, you can accomplish great things. I think coming to my library gives people a good start."

If you'd like to start *your* own library, find an area in your house (or garage) that's easily accessible—and one your family won't mind sharing with the public! Check out garage or yard sales for inexpensive bookshelves, or build your own by placing sturdy boards on top of stacked bricks. Stock your library with books and magazines you find at garage and tag sales, used-book stores, or solicit donations (of reading materials) from neighbors, friends, local schools, and public libraries that are giving away old books.

Would you like to volunteer at a *public* library? Most are short-staffed these days and welcome students who work as "pages" after school and on weekends, keeping books neatly arranged on shelves, taking care of paperwork, etc. Give your area library a call for more info.

He's Having a Ball!

JOSHUA RAIFORD

Joshua Raiford is one of those enterprising kids who "sees a need and fills it." His neighborhood, in the Harlem area of New York City, didn't have a Little League baseball team, and in 1989, with the help of his mom and dad, Joshua founded the Harlem Little League for kids in the community.

"I was 8 at the time," says Joshua, now 11, "and I noticed that two of my friends wore baseball uniforms to school. I asked why, and they explained they had Little League practice. I told my mom *I'd* like to join a team and she checked around our neighborhood to find the nearest one. But there weren't any. The *closest* Little League was about 30 blocks away, and I was out of the district, so I couldn't join it."

Joshua made a deal with his mom: he promised to take piano lessons (and practice regularly) if she agreed to help him start a Little League team. "She had to write to Little League head-quarters for an application, then we had to find sponsors (local businesses) for each team we formed," recalls Joshua. He adds that he, his mother, and two of his friends were interviewed by an area newspaper at the start of the project. "Parents in the neighborhood read the article and wrote to us asking if their kids could join the teams," he says. Word about Harlem Little League spread rapidly, and soon 129 boys and girls had signed up for the eight teams (today 450 kids play on the 34 teams in the league, and Joshua and his parents have also started Harlem *Soccer* League, which boasts eight teams and 120 kids).

Organizing a Little League has taken a lot of work and dedication, according to Joshua, who gives much of the credit to his parents. "Sometimes I feel bad that they have to put in so much of their time [doing administrative work, overseeing 'sign-ups,' etc.]. They both have full-time jobs, too," he says, "so that doesn't leave them much time for themselves."

But Joshua adds that Harlem Little League has been a very rewarding experience for him and the other kids—and the adults—in the community. "We've gotten a lot of help from people, especially the businesses that sponsor the teams," he says. "And each of the kids has made a lot of good new friends over the past few years."

Would you like to start a Little League in your community? For details, contact Little League Baseball, Inc., P.O. Box 3485, Williamsport, PA 17701; 717-326-1921.

Crime-Fighting Kids

LINDA WARSAW

"I was 12 when I decided to start 'Kids Against Crime,'" says 19-year-old Linda Warsaw, of Devore, California. "Our house had been burglarized, and as a result, my mother started volunteering at the Victim-Witness Assistance Program run by the San Bernardino district attorney's office. She and I had always been close, so I became a volunteer, too."

Through her work at the DA's office, Linda learned about hard-core crimes committed against children. "I heard the attorneys talking about their cases, which dealt with everything from child molestation, child abuse, kidnapping, and child pornography to murder," Linda recalls. "I couldn't believe kids were the victims of such horrible crimes, so I decided to go to court and actually hear the children testify during certain cases. After watching a case that dealt with an eight-year-old who had been molested by a neighborhood baby-sitter, I knew I had to do *something.*"

Linda started by asking herself *why* kids are such easy targets, why they're prone to victimization in the first place. "The answer is that kids just don't know how to *handle* certain situations. In most cases, kids are victimized by people they know and trust and love. I wanted to educate children to help prevent them from becoming victims."

Eleven volunteers attended the first meeting of Kids Against Crime (KAC). During the past seven years, the organization has grown rapidly, and today there are 4,500 members nationwide (most KAC chapters are based in schools).

KAC volunteers speak at schools and crime-prevention fairs; they also hold workshops on crimes against children, telling kids how they can protect themselves—and how to get help if they *are* victimized.

"We present skits for younger kids," adds Linda. "We realized that little children can't sit through a two-hour presentation by a law enforcement agent, or rape crisis counselor, or child-abuse specialist. Small children respond well to 'visuals,' so we wrote plays that deal with topics like coping with school bullies, the dangers of smoking or doing drugs, child abuse, kidnapping, etc. The effect of these skits is phenomenal. Afterwards, little children recite what they've learned to keep from becoming victims."

KAC members are also trained by law enforcement agencies to fingerprint children at schools, malls, and fairs. "We've fingerprinted more than 20,000 kids," Linda notes. "And if one of those children gets lost or is missing, his or her parents will have a copy of the child's fingerprints to give to law enforcement agents to help them in their search."

In addition, KAC provides a hotline (1-800-KAC-5670). "It's for kids who just feel lonely and need somebody to talk with, kids who are victims of incest or abuse or other crimes, kids who have family problems or have run away. We *aren't* a crisis-intervention line; we just listen [hotline volunteers are specially trained by various agencies]. If a kid calls and says he's

Linda Warsaw.

on drugs or having family problems, we're equipped to refer him to the agency that can help him. We try to convince kids to get the professional help they need."

To support KAC activities and services, the organization holds regular bowl-a-thons and car washes. "But most of our money comes from grants," says Linda, who, along with other volunteers, has "learned the fine art of grant writing! Our first major grant came from Ronald McDonald Children's Charities. Also, the city of San Bernardino assists with funding." A portion of KAC funds pays for rent. "We operated out of the district attorney's office for the first year," says Linda. "But our membership grew so quickly, we had to rent our own *building.*"

Many KAC members have themselves been victims of crimes, according to Linda. "One member was abandoned by her parents when she was three. She was adopted by her grandparents; then, when she was eight, her grandfather raped her. The grandparents abandoned this girl when she was 11, and since then, she went from foster home to foster home (sometimes three in one month).

"People blamed her for everything; they labeled her a 'troubled child,' they called her a 'good-for-nothing kid,' and she started believing them. She became suicidal, attempted to run away, and almost flunked out of school. Then, one day she and some other kids were hanging out at a park where KAC was sponsoring a crime-prevention fair. The girl decided to get fingerprinted, then asked about the organization and what we do. She told us *her* story, and we contacted her foster parents. She became very involved in KAC, performing in skits, visiting schools, etc. Her self-esteem has improved *so much.* She was praised for the work she was doing and she started to feel good about herself. And she felt good because she was helping to prevent other kids from going through what she'd experienced," says Linda.

"KAC recognizes that kids have a great need for love and attention—and the opportunity to help others. We stress how important the children are, and how much power they have."

Would you like to start a Kids Against Crime chapter at your school or in your community? For information (including a KAC newsletter and crime-prevention tips), write to Kids Against Crime, P.O. Box 22004, San Bernardino, CA 92406. Enclose a self-addressed, stamped, business-size envelope.

Ms. Sussal Goes to Washington
JENNIFER SUSSAL

"Anytime I really wanted to do something, I did it," says Jennifer Faith Sussal. That kind of motivation, coupled with a knack for "being persuasive," and a keen desire to help others, propelled the Rockville Centre, New York, girl into the world of politics, and in 1988, Jennifer became the only teenager to testify before a Senate committee, when she successfully lobbied for a bill requiring warning labels on alcoholic beverages.

"I've been working in the field of alcohol abuse since I was 15," says Jennifer, now 21 and a graduate student at Johns Hopkins School of Public Health, in Baltimore. "I was very upset by what I was seeing in my community—all the drunk-driving fatalities, as well as other effects of alcohol and drug abuse. I was seeing people my own age dying by the hundreds because of drunk-driving accidents."

Jennifer eventually became president of her school's anti-DWI (driving while intoxicated) group. The organization grew quickly from 23 members to 350 and "we started doing incredible things with the community, organizing parades and school assemblies—all sorts of public-awareness programs," says Jennifer.

She says that "this type of work was extremely fulfilling," even *before* she was thrust into the national spotlight. "Then, four or five months into my involvement in this field, while I was going to elementary and secondary schools where I gave speeches about the dangers of drinking and driving, I came up with the idea of a warning label for alcoholic beverages. I'd seen warning labels on just about everything else, from bubble bath to various foods, and I wondered why there was no written warning on *alcohol.*"

Today, Jennifer laughs when she recalls her first efforts at "lobbying" for her cause. "I called the alcohol companies and said, 'Hi, my name is Jennifer, and I want you to know people in my community are dying because of drunk-driving accidents. Would you please put a warning label on your products?'

"Of course, the companies didn't take me seriously," says Jennifer, who then started calling area politicians to garner support. "At one point, I had a phone bill running into the hundreds of dollars!" She also compiled a 70-page book, filled with statistics about drunk-driving accidents, as well as letters from people who supported her efforts, plus a list of organizations committed to preventing alcohol abuse. "Finally, in my research, I came upon a Washington, D.C., lobbying group called the Center for Science in the Public Interest. It was one of those chance phone calls that paid off. I spoke with a woman named Pat Taylor, who happened to be working on a campaign to put warning labels on alcohol containers.

"From my research, I'd already discovered that 'my idea' wasn't new. Senator Strom Thurmond (Rep.-SC) had started introducing bills for warning labels as early as 1969 (and I wasn't even born then!). Pat explained that Senator Thurmond had a bill for warning labels up in 1987. I was so excited." The

Center for Science and other lobbying groups invited Jennifer and her high school principal, Robin Calitri, to travel to D.C. to speak at a coalition meeting (made up of dozens of lobbying groups, politicians, etc.). On that and following trips to Washington, Jennifer acted as the youth spokesperson for various lobbying groups (the American Medical Association, the PTA, and other organizations were actively lobbying for passage of the bill).

"I met with senators and congressional representatives, or their staffs, and tried to convince them to vote *for* the bill. In an issue like this, it's very difficult for a congressperson or senator to say no to a teen lobbyist—especially when the media is focusing attention on her," says Jennifer, who adds that she honed her lobbying skills quickly. "I developed a very polished, convincing approach and I went around to everyone on Capitol Hill who would see me. I also kept accurate, thorough records of whom I had talked with."

During this time, Jennifer continued to speak at high schools, encouraging students to start letter-writing campaigns in support of the bill. "I spent 10 to 15 hours a day working for its passage," she adds. "I don't know how I managed to go to school—or graduate!"

In 1988, Jennifer was asked to testify before the Senate Committee on Science, Commerce and Transportation. "It was very exciting," she says. "I couldn't believe it was happening. I spoke for about 10 minutes, citing statistics about drunk-driving fatalities, refuting contradictory research put out by the alcohol industry, and in general telling why I, as a young person, felt the warning label was necessary. I felt I had everyone's attention, and I also felt as though I was speaking for young people in this country. I was so happy I was able to speak for young people, because that's where the problem with alcohol abuse is most prevalent."

Jennifer with *(from left to right),* Robin Calitri, her high school principal,
Senator Strom Thurmond (R.-SC), and David Goldban, lobbyist.

The bill on warning labels was passed, as part of the Omnibus Drug Act of 1988, and went into effect in January of 1989. Today, every alcoholic beverage sold in the United States must carry a label cautioning that: (1) according to the Surgeon General, women should not drink alcoholic beverages during pregnancy because of the risk of birth defects; and (2) consumption of alcoholic beverages impairs your ability to drive a car or operate machinery, and may cause health problems.

Today, Jennifer has her undergraduate degree in public health/political science and is working on a master's degree in public health. Next year, she plans to enter medical school "because I feel that by becoming a doctor, I can make an even greater contribution in the area of public health and alcohol-abuse prevention." (She's also considering attending *law school* after she completes medical school!)

Jennifer has also served on numerous alcohol-abuse organization boards and is currently national youth representative for RID (Remove Intoxicated Drivers). In addition, she's on the board of directors of the National Coalition to Prevent Impaired Driving. "We just had a big meeting in Colorado," says Jennifer, "and we're involved in many exciting projects." Among those projects Jennifer is working on: attempting to convince medical schools to include alcohol awareness/prevention training in their curricula; lobbying for lowering the "legal" blood alcohol level in drivers under 21 from .1 to .02; working with coaches at major colleges and universities to limit the amount of alcohol advertisements at sporting events, and to develop alcohol-awareness programs to eliminate the association between alcohol and sports; and lobbying for passage of a bill requiring warnings in alcohol print or TV ads. ("For example, if a beer ad is shown on TV, a warning would be displayed on the screen after the ad has aired," explains Jennifer.)

Jennifer also continues to speak to students (from elementary school through college) about the dangers of drunk driving. "I do role playing with the students," she adds. "I hold a set of keys in my hand and pretend I'm drunk. Then I challenge the students to take the keys away from me. I try to get people to realize the *power* they have. You *can* do something to stop a person from driving drunk. You *can* take away his keys, or let the air out of his tires. You *can* make a difference if you really want to."

Want to get involved in your local, state, or federal government?

1. If you're interested in a particular issue, and would like to have something enacted into law, contact your state and federal senators and congresspersons. Ask for the names of other senators or representatives serving on committees that pertain to your area of concern.

2. Check with your state senators or representatives to find out about internship programs (many local governments sponsor internship programs; some are available on the national level).

3. Volunteer to work on political campaigns.

4. If possible, visit your state capital, or Washington, D.C., and make an appointment to see your state's elected representatives.

Would you like to get involved in the "war on drunk driving"? Contact these organizations for info:

RID (Remove Intoxicated Drivers)
P.O. Box 520
Schenectady, NY 12301

National Coalition to Prevent Impaired Driving
1730 Rhode Island Avenue, N.W.
Suite 600
Washington, D.C. 20036

Rescuing the Environment, Saving Animals' Lives

Kory Johnson

Kristin Johnson

Casey Golden

Lyle Solla-Yates

Lauren Krohn

Cleaning Up the Environment

KORY JOHNSON

When Kory Johnson was 9, her 16-year-old sister died. "My mother drank contaminated water when she was pregnant with Amy," explains Kory, now 13, "and that's what caused my sister to get sick."

After Amy's death, Kory's mom started attending various environmental group meetings and Kory "tagged along." Prompted by what she learned at the meetings, Kory founded Children for a Safe Environment in 1988, and she and a handful of other kids from her Phoenix, Arizona, community set out to clean up the environment. One of their first projects? A war on Styrofoam cups and containers!

"We wrote to Mrs. Kroc, the owner of McDonald's, and asked that the restaurants stop using Styrofoam products," Kory recalls. Mrs. Kroc wrote back, saying that the corporation was exploring the possibility of *recycling* Styrofoam containers. But Kory and her pals weren't satisfied. They contacted the Greenpeace organization in San Diego, California, and together the two groups gathered all the Styrofoam containers they could stuff into several refrigerator boxes and shipped them to Mrs. Kroc. "She ended up with a front yard full of Styrofoam!" says Kory.

Seven months after the kids began their "no Styrofoam" campaign, McDonald's banned the material from its restaurants.

Not long after the "McDonald's victory," Kory's group took on a powerful Phoenix area corporation that planned to burn hazardous waste ("They were going to ship most of the waste in from other states," says Kory). The kids staged a protest at the incinerator site, appeared on TV news and talk shows (including *Geraldo*), and mailed thousands of fliers to Phoenix residents.

"At first, there were only five of us, sitting around a table licking stamps and sealing fliers," says Kory. "It was a lot of work, but many people in our area had no idea that a company planned to burn hazardous waste in their community, and we had to let them know." After a year, hundreds of concerned citizens got involved, staging protests and sit-ins at the site. "It was a tough fight," Kory admits—because the Arizona state government had agreed to allow the incinerator to operate. "We raised $44 million in taxpayers' money, enough to pay to the incinerator company so they'd leave," she says. "It was a lot of money, but people were willing to pay it to get the company out. If $44 million could save even 44 lives, it was worth it."

Today, there are more than 300 members of Children for a Safe Environment. "We have branches at other area schools," says Kory, "and when we need to work together on a big project, I contact the heads of these groups." (The core group holds planning meetings on a regular basis, and representatives from other schools attend.)

Although Kory is still very involved in environmental work,

Kory Johnson.

she has recently focused her attention on helping the homeless as well. She and other volunteers collect blankets, clothing, food, and bottled water and take these supplies to homeless shelters and street people.

But whatever problem Kory takes on, one thing is clear to the residents of Phoenix, Arizona: Kory Johnson is truly a "kid who cares"!

What can *you* do to "save" our earth? Start by instituting a recycling program at home (separating cans and newspapers from regular garbage, for example). Encourage your school to launch a recycling program (concentrate on the cafeteria). Stop using Styrofoam cups and containers; instead, opt for reusable ceramic mugs and dishes. Carry a thermos—instead of "juice boxes."

Check your local newspaper to find out about environmental organizations and their activities—then volunteer!

For more info about what you can do to safeguard our environment, contact these organizations: American Forestry Association, 1-800-368-5748; Greenpeace USA, 1436 U Street, N.W., Washington, D.C., 20036, 202-466-2823; National Audubon Society, 950 Third Avenue, New York, NY 10022, 212-832-3200; National Recycling Coalition, 1101 30th Street, N.W., Suite 305, Washington, D.C. 20007, 202-625-6406; the Sierra Club, 730 Polk Street, San Francisco, CA 94109, 415-776-2211.

And be sure to check out one of the best "environment-friendly" books in print, *50 Simple Things You Can Do to Save the Earth,* by the EarthWorks Group, EarthWorks Press.

Rallying Support
for Rain Forests

KRISTIN JOHNSON

Did you know that . . .

- Although tropical rain forests cover only 7 percent of the earth's land surface, they're home to 50 percent of all plant and animal species?
- Tropical rain forests are the earth's oldest continuous eco-system—and some in Southeast Asia have existed for more than 70 million years?
- A typical four-square-mile patch of rain forest contains as many as 1,500 flowering plant species, 750 tree species, 400 bird species, 150 butterfly species, 125 mammal species, and 100 reptile species?
- Plants in tropical rain forests are a valuable source of medicines, including some anticancer drugs?

These are just a few of the interesting facts students learn during one of 18-year-old Kristin Johnson's presentations on the world's tropical rain forests.

The Woodinville, Washington, teen became interested in conservation issues in the ninth grade, when she put together a slide presentation on tropical rain forests as part of a science project. "The presentation lasted an hour, and I was invited to show the slides at a nearby elementary school," says Kristin. "It was fun—and I was discovering that tropical rain forests are pretty neat places which form a 'green belt' around the equator. The forests have an annual rainfall of between 120 and 400 inches, and the year-round temperature is 75 to 80 degrees, which allows for a wide diversity of plant and animal life (animals can breed all year round)."

Kristin adds that the United States has one tropical rain forest—in Hawaii. Other tropical rain forests exist in Africa, South America, Central America, Southeast Asia, and Australia. "I also learned that they're being destroyed at a rapid rate," she notes (for a variety of reasons, including cattle ranching, industrialization, development farming, and logging for hardwood; approximately 50 to 100 acres disappear *every minute*).

During the next few years, Kristin spoke to more than 3,000 schoolchildren about the magic—and plight—of tropical rain forests. "Then, when I started volunteering at the Woodland Park Zoo [in Seattle], I met Scott Barton, a keeper who happened to have worked on a [rain forest] reserve in Colombia." Together, Kristin and Scott came up with the idea of "adopting" a Colombian rain forest and launched the "Adopt an Acre" program.

"I wanted to get more kids interested in rain forests in general, as well as raise money to support the Colombian reserve, but I needed to make my presentation at *so many* schools there was no way I could do it alone," says Kristin. "So, a bunch of friends and I formed a group called R.A.I.N. (Rainforest Awareness Information Network), and all 12 of us started making presentations."

During the past two years, the group has raised enough

Kristin Johnson.

money to save 650 acres of Colombian rain forest. "Each acre costs $40 (one-half acre, $20). Our goal is to raise $100,000," Kristin explains. The money goes to the Puget Sound Chapter of the American Association of Zookeepers, which works with a nonprofit Colombian conservation/education organization.

The R.A.I.N. presentation is available to students around the country ("Anyone can write to us for a copy of the script," says Kristin. "We can't provide slides, though, since ours are owned and copyrighted by scientists around the world"). Kristin and Scott Barton have also put together a comprehensive "teacher's guide," which they send to interested educators. Called *Rainforest Conservation: Empowering Youth Through Conservation Action,* the well-researched and professional-quality guide includes amazing rain forest facts, and information on a variety of activities, such as fund raising, outreach and awareness projects, games, art projects, and an extensive bibliography of books and tapes.

This fall, when Kristin enters college ("I plan to major in zoology at the University of Washington," she says), she intends to remain active in R.A.I.N. "We had a meeting recently to discuss what will happen when the seniors leave for college. Everyone is very excited about continuing the group next year!"

Would you like to know more about the Adopt an Acre program? For info, write to AAZK, Woodland Park Zoo, 5500 Phinney Avenue, Seattle, WA 98103.

For a copy of the R.A.I.N. script, or the teacher's guide, *Rainforest Conservation,* write to: Rainforest Awareness Information Network, 18802 185th Avenue, N.E., Woodinville, WA 98072.

Making Products "Earth-Friendly"

CASEY GOLDEN

When Casey Golden, of Evergreen, Colorado, was 10, he invented a biodegradable golf tee.

"One of my teachers had given our class an assignment to come up with a problem, then solve it," says Casey. *"My* biggest problem at the time was having to pick up my dad's broken golf tees when I caddied for him." (Casey's dad, John, had explained that tees left on the course could dull or damage lawnmower blades.)

"I wondered why someone couldn't invent a golf tee that just 'disappeared' into the ground when the sprinklers went on or it rained," says Casey, who decided to create a "dissolvable" tee himself. Using a mixture of flour, peat moss, fertilizer, old newspapers, grass seed, and applesauce, he developed a "biodegradable" tee that was strong enough to support a golf ball, but soft enough to dissolve and be absorbed by the soil.

Casey entered his tee in Invent America (a nationwide contest for kids, grades K-8) and won $1,000. But that was only the beginning of his success story. Together with his father, Casey formed a company, Biodynamics, which makes and sells the

Casey Golden.

earth-friendly Bio-T. "We had to test a lot of variations on the original formula," says Casey, adding that golf course owners weren't thrilled about the grass seed component since they didn't want "strange" grass sprouting on their pristine greens!

Casey and his dad worked with a group of chemists to perfect the recipe for Bio-T, and, today, Casey's company sells the tees to environment-conscious golf courses, pro shops, and sporting goods stores.

Biodegradable tees benefit the earth in several ways, according to Casey. First, they eliminate the "litter" that results when golfers fail to pick up used tees. "The tees also help save trees," adds Casey. "If every golfer in the country used biodegradable tees, we'd save 40,000 45-foot-high birch trees a year [most tees are made from birch wood]. We'd also prevent about 400 tons of newspaper from being dumped in landfills annually," he notes, "since we use recycled paper in the Bio-T to give it strength." Casey also points out that his tee actually benefits the soil. "Since it's absorbed by the ground, it acts as a kind of mulch that holds water and helps the grass to grow better," he explains.

Currently, Casey is working on another biodegradable product—one that will deliver nutrients to plants and control the amount of water each plant receives. "Most plants die because of over- or underwatering," says Casey. "They develop 'root rot' if they get *too* much water." Casey's new invention will hold water and deliver it to plants in the right amounts.

When Casey isn't busy inventing, he's involved in after-school activities, such as basketball and golf. He also travels throughout the country, making presentations at schools. "Usually, I talk about Invent America and how kids can come up with ideas for inventions. I also talk about environmental issues; I'm a member of the National Arbor Day Foundation [an organization devoted to preserving existing trees and planting new ones]. I tell how I received 10 saplings from the foundation, which I planted around my house." (Casey and an environmental group at his junior high also raised funds to buy and plant trees, shrubs, and flowers around the school.)

"I'd like to see more people working on products that are safe for our environment," says Casey. "Kids (or grownups) could look at an *existing* product and ask themselves if there's a way it could be changed so it helped, instead of harmed, the environment. We need to become much more environment-conscious when we invent new products—or make changes in older ones," he says.

Would you like to learn more about the Invent America contest?

Write or call Invent America at

510 King St., Suite 420

Alexandria, VA 22314

703-684-1836

Are you interested in joining the National Arbor Day Foundation—and helping to save our precious trees?

Contact the organization at

211 North 12th St.

Lincoln, NE 68508

402-474-5655

Want to become "environment conscious"? Join CAPE (Children's Alliance for Protection of the Environment), P.O. Box 307, Austin, TX 78767; 512-476-2273. Membership is free—and so is CAPE's newspaper, *Many Hands,* written by and for kids.

A "Pal" of the Wildlife

LYLE SOLLA-YATES

Ten-year-old Lyle Solla-Yates is a big fan of manatees, or "sea cows," an endangered aquatic mammal living off the coast of Florida. "Manatees look kind of like very big gray fish with a walrus face and whiskers," says Lyle, who lives in Miami. "They're gentle and friendly to people," he adds, noting that he's patted a manatee at a Florida seaquarium ("It wanted to be fed. Manatees eat plants that grow in the water, but at a seaquarium, they also feed on lettuce").

Though these herbivorous creatures pose no threat to humans, *people* are their number-one enemy. Only 1,500 manatees exist in the United States today, and they're fighting for their lives. "People drive over them with speedboats," explains Lyle, "and the motor blades cut into their skin, injuring or killing them. We also dump lots of garbage and poisonous materials from landfills into the ocean, and the manatees eat these wastes or breathe them in, and they get very sick and die." Most people don't know that manatees aren't just "gentle giants." They also help keep our streams and rivers free of unwanted aquatic plants that clog waterways. Manatees feed

Lyle Solla-Yates; pictured above is "Pals of Wildlife."

on these plants (one manatee can gobble up 60 to 100 pounds of plants per day!).

In 1989, Lyle founded "Pals of Wildlife," an organization devoted to raising funds to help save the manatee (today, Pals raises money to save other endangered species as well, such as whales, koalas, and the Florida panther, and the organization divides its proceeds between Save the Manatees, Greenpeace, and the Children's Rainforest Project).

The group—which started out with 5 kids and has grown to 40—raises between $100 and $500 per year. "We set up booths at fairs and sell craft items," says Lyle, "as well as T-shirts, pencils, and buttons carrying the Pals logo, with the motto: "When animals die, we're dead meat."

Pals also held an Earthday Birthday party to raise funds. "We had birthday cakes and sold arts and crafts items. We also planted trees in a local park."

Lyle and his "pals" agree that their work is well worth the time and effort. "We may never see or get to know an individual animal we've helped save, but knowing we *did* save an animal is our reward," he says.

Want to "adopt" a manatee? For information, write to: Save the Manatee Club, 500 North Maitland Avenue, Maitland, FL 32751, or call 1-800-432-JOIN.

Interested in adopting *another* endangered species? Contact: Adopt a Species and Its Habitat, Department AS, National Wildlife Federation, 8925 Leesburg Pike, Vienna, VA 22184. This organization offers a kit ($5) that tells you how to adopt an endangered species *and* its habitat (the place it lives).

Helping Our
Four-Footed Friends

LAUREN KROHN

Lauren Krohn, 18, can't have a pet—one with *fur*, that is. If Lauren spends too much time around a dog or cat, she starts to wheeze and sneeze, her eyes get red and itchy, and she may even break out in an unsightly rash! Lauren is allergic to animal hair, but she loves furry creatures all the same—and that's why she devotes much of her time to making her Scarsdale, New York, community aware of issues involved in the animal rights movement, as well as raising funds to see that cats and dogs who are housed in several area shelters are well taken care of.

For the past two years, Lauren has served as president of H.E.L.P. Animals (High school Effort for the Love and Protection of Animals) at Scarsdale High. Now a senior, Lauren notes that she joined H.E.L.P. four years ago, when she learned about the organization in French class. "My French teacher, Laura Bell, is adviser to the group, and she mentioned animal rights and H.E.L.P. from time to time in class," Lauren explains. "I decided to join because I thought it would be a good way to get involved in community work and help animals at the same time."

The club, which has a strong core membership of 30, but often attracts 40 or 50 students to its twice-a-month meetings, has two goals, according to Lauren: the first is to provide food and services to three animal shelters (in the nearby communities of New Rochelle, Yonkers, and Elmsford). The second is to educate Scarsdale students and the community at large about animal rights issues and suggest ways people can treat animals more humanely.

"The club sponsors lectures that are open to the community," says Lauren, "and we invite speakers who talk about a variety of animal rights issues—everything from the need for reform in factory farming, in which livestock or chickens are forced to live in unsanitary, overcrowded conditions, to alternatives to the dissection of animals in high school biology classes)." Through word-of-mouth campaigns, the group also lets the community know that area shelters need certain supplies, such as old carpets and blankets (to make pets more comfortable), newspapers, and dog and cat food. "We set up boxes in the school for donations," says Lauren.

In addition, H.E.L.P. tries to make people more aware of the need to neuter or spay pets (to curb the huge numbers of unwanted puppies and kittens that are abandoned each year in the United States). The organization has donated funds to one shelter, with the proviso that the money be used to spay or neuter animals that are adopted.

H.E.L.P. members also spend many hours of free time at the Yonkers shelter, cleaning cages, exercising and feeding pets, and "doing basically what the regular staff attendants do," adds Lauren.

The students devote a great deal of time and effort to fund-raising projects, including potluck suppers and bake sales (the regular lecture series also generates donations). "One of our

Lauren, with H.E.L.P. vice president Clarissa Tang.

biggest projects is an annual bake sale held during Scarsdale's Halloween window-painting contest," says Lauren. "We get 40 or 50 students to bake things and we make between $600 and $800 every year."

The group tackled its most challenging project last April—a large antiques and collectibles fair, held at the high school. "We started working on the fair six months in advance," says Lauren, adding that the group had an "antiques expert" who gave them valuable advice. "Mrs. Bell is involved in the antiques business," Lauren explains. The club placed ads in numerous New York area newspapers, the local *Pennysaver,* and a Connecticut antiques newsletter, in order to attract vendors or dealers. Forty vendors bought tables or spaces (for booths), and H.E.L.P. raised $1,500. The Westchester/Putnam United Way program, Youth in Philanthropy, had offered to match profits up to $1,000, so H.E.L.P. ended up with $2,500, most of which they donated to the Yonkers Animal Shelter, with the excess going to another organization, Forgotten Felines. The shelter agreed to use the money to build additional pens, so they can care for more animals and "won't have to euthanize them," says Lauren, who adds that the shelter also plans to spend some of the money to refurbish existing pens "to make the animals more comfortable."

Despite her fur allergy, Lauren visits area shelters several times a year to find out what they need—as well as to see the animals the organization is helping. "It can be heartbreaking," she says of the hundreds of cats and dogs in need of homes. "But it's also a constant source of inspiration. Visiting the shelters gives me and other H.E.L.P. members the incentive to continue our work, to see that the environment of the shelters is comfortable, and to make sure as many animals as possible can be well cared for until they're adopted."

Would you like to learn more about animal rights—or spend a few hours a week helping our furry friends? For info, contact the national headquarters of the A.S.P.C.A. (American Society for the Prevention of Cruelty to Animals), at 212-876-7700, or the Humane Society of the United States, at 202-452-1100, or call the local branches of these organizations.

Also, consider volunteering at area shelters, feeding, bathing, or exercising the animals. Check with shelters to find out what supplies they need (most welcome small rugs, blankets, newspapers, and dog and cat food)—then work with other students at your school, church, or temple to sponsor a communitywide collection.

Bringing Help to the Homeless and Needy, Companionship to the Elderly

Trevor Ferrell

Justin Lebo

Michelle Ondako

David Cox

Hero to the Homeless

TREVOR FERRELL

In 1983, when Trevor Ferrell was 11, he was shocked by a TV news report about homeless people in his area. Trevor had thought "people lived on the streets" only in places like India—not in America. And certainly not in the America *he* knew. Trevor (now 20), had grown up in a 16-room house with a swimming pool, surrounded by two acres of woods.

When Trevor's dad, Frank, confirmed that people did indeed live on the streets in America—and in nearby Philadelphia, in fact—Trevor badgered his parents until they agreed to drive him to Philadelphia's inner city, where homeless people gathered in doorways, trying to stay warm. He took a blanket and his favorite pillow with him, and gave them to a man the family found curled up on a grate.

That was the beginning of Trevor's mission to Philadelphia's more than 20,000 homeless. Several nights a week, the Ferrells drove into the city, taking more blankets and clothing, which they distributed to the street people. Soon, they began to provide hot meals as well. When local TV stations found out about Trevor's work and featured him on their news shows, people started donating money—enough for Trevor and his family to open a shelter called Trevor's Place. Trevor Ferrell was, suddenly, a regular on the streets—and the homeless people he helped nicknamed him "Little Jesus."

What began as a simple gesture—a boy giving a blanket and pillow to a homeless man in 1983—has, over the years, evolved into a major, independent, nonprofit organization. Today, Trevor's Campaign is run by a national advisory board and a professional staff, and supported by hundreds of volunteers. The campaign sponsors two homes, including Trevor's Place and Trevor's Next Door, which house 84 kids and adults and have private rooms for families. (Trevor's Next Door received a start-up grant from the Department of Housing and Urban Development, and $50,000 from McKinney Act funds.)

In addition to the residential homes, the campaign runs Trevor's Thrift Shop, which generates revenue for the shelters. Trevor's Campaign also provides job-skills training and employment counseling, health services (an on-site medical facility is staffed by a doctor), and a child care and child development service (the child care/learning center service is open nine hours a day, five days a week, so parents can work or attend job-skills classes. Child development and parenting-skills programs are also offered).

Trevor's organization also continues its "nightly food runs," which the boy and his family started nine years ago, and the homeless on Philadelphia's streets are served a nutritious, hot meal by volunteers.

Until he started college a year ago, Trevor spent between 60 and 70 hours a week working at the two residences or the thrift shop, and taking part in public relations ventures to raise money for the campaign. He's also garnered his share of awards and honors. Mother Teresa invited him to visit India to

Trevor Ferrell.

join her mission to that country's poor, and Trevor has traveled there twice. He's addressed the United Nations and attended a conference on homelessness in Africa. Trevor was also the subject of a made-for-TV movie, *Christmas on Division Street* (a project initiated by Steven Spielberg, who has said that Trevor's concern for the homeless reminded him of the boy who rescued the extraterrestrial in the movie *E.T.*).

Today, Trevor is a sophomore at Cabrini College, in Radnor, Pennsylvania, and though he's not a day-to-day fixture at Trevor's Place and Trevor's Next Door, his presence and inspiration are keenly felt by the many volunteers, and, of course, the homeless and formerly homeless people he's helped clothe, feed, and shelter over the years.

Would you like to learn more about Trevor's Campaign—or make a donation to help Philadelphia's homeless population? Call 1-800-TREVORS, or write to: Trevor's Campaign for the Homeless, 3415 West Chester Pike, Newtown Square, PA 19073.

Interested in *starting* a soup kitchen or shelter? Work with kids and adults from your school, church, or temple to make your dream a reality. Visit successful shelters and soup kitchens in other towns, asking the administrators for advice about fund raising and general operating procedures. For more tips—and inspiration—check out a copy of *Trevor's Place: The Story of the Boy Who Brings Hope to the Homeless* (by Frank and Janet Ferrell, with Edward Wakin, HarperCollins).

For more info about helping to feed, clothe, and house the homeless in our nation, contact these organizations: Food for the Hungry, P.O. Box E, Scottsdale, AZ 85260, 1-800-2-HUNGER; Habitat for Humanity, Habitat and Church Streets, Americus, GA 31709, 912-924-6935; National Coalition for the Homeless, 1621 Connecticut Avenue, N.W., Suite 400, Washington, D.C. 20009, 202-265-2371; USA HARVEST, 1-800-872-4366 (this organization collects and distributes 30 million pounds of food to the homeless in 23 states every year).

Would you like to *volunteer* at a shelter or soup kitchen in your neighborhood? Call the American Red Cross, Salvation Army, and area temples and churches to find out if they sponsor food and shelter programs.

Consider organizing a "food run" to deliver hot meals to street people. You'll need a van, a licensed driver, and an adult to supervise your operation (a licensed registered dietitian can give you pointers on safe, nutritious foods to prepare). Ask volunteers to cook and pack meals, as well as make deliveries.

Ask area shelter directors what their residents need, then organize a communitywide "supplies drive." During the winter, the homeless need coats, warm scarves, hats, socks, and gloves, and sturdy boots and shoes. Shelters are always in need of "personal" items like toothpaste, soap, shampoo, sheets, pillowcases, towels, and washcloths. Hold fund raisers at school (or your church or temple) and use the money to buy new items in bulk from wholesalers.

Making Old Bikes New Again

JUSTIN LEBO

Justin Lebo got into the habit of giving at an early age. "When I was four or five, my family donated toys, clothing, and food to a local orphanage twice a year," explains the Saddle Brook, New Jersey, boy, now 15.

But when the family moved to a new area, they weren't able to make their regular visits to the orphanage. Justin continued the family tradition of "doing for others" with his own project—buying and restoring old bikes and giving them to needy kids.

"I'd bought a used bike for $6 at a garage sale. I fixed it up really nice. Then I bought another old bike and fixed it. I wasn't using either bike, though, because I already had two store-bought bicycles." Justin decided to donate his refurbished bikes to a local boys' home. "When I saw how happy the two kids were who got the bikes, I decided to buy and fix bicycles for the *other* 22 kids at the home," he recalls.

Over the past four years, Justin has restored more than 150 bikes for "just about any kid who'd like a bicycle and can't afford one." At first, Justin used his own money to buy parts

Justin Lebo.

and accessories for the bikes, but after local newspapers ran several stories about Justin and his cause, people started sending monetary donations. "Actually, I just wanted old bikes," says Justin, but he adds that the money has come in handy. "Sometimes I hear about a group of kids who need bikes, but I can't find any old ones to fix up. So I use the money to buy them new ones," he explains. "And I bought new *tricycles* for a group of kids who have AIDS," he says. "They were just too little to ride bikes."

Although Justin was recently named "A Point of Light" as part of President George Bush's Thousand Points of Light Foundation project, which honors Americans who help others, the teen says his real reward comes from making kids happy. "One time, I fixed up 15 bikes as gifts for kids attending a Christmas party at a local church," says Justin. "When I delivered the bikes, the priest asked me to stay for the party, but I decided not to. Having the kids thank me in person wasn't necessary. To know I did something to make them happy was thanks enough."

Want to find—and fix up—old bikes for needy kids? Check out garage and yard sales, as well as the classified ads in your local newspaper. Run an inexpensive ad in the community *Pennysaver* asking for donations of used bikes and tricycles, as well as spare parts and accessories. Ask your local bike shop for any spare parts they can't use.

Donate your "like new" bikes to halfway houses, homeless shelters, churches, and recreation centers.

Kids, Caring, and Companionship

MICHELLE ONDAKO

When Michelle Ondako was assigned an independent educational project during her junior year in high school, she decided to "do something on volunteerism.

"I wanted to find a way teens could help people, especially the older residents in our community. Kids don't get much 'good press' when it comes to helping others," says the Lower Burrell, Pennsylvania, teen.

As part of her project, Michelle founded S.H.O.P.—Students Helping Older People. "We started with 10 volunteers," she recalls, "but when I graduated in 1991, there were 25 members." (Today, S.H.O.P. boasts 53 members, and because Michelle is away at college—she's a sophomore at Georgetown University—her 17-year-old sister, Kristin, now heads up the organization.)

"When we first began, we were basically trying to get the older people to trust us, to let us into their houses. [The group posted notices at the local center for the aging and at high-rise apartment buildings that house many seniors.] We helped them with yard work, grocery shopping, cleaning, cooking, and

Michelle Ondako.

moving heavy things like furniture. But our real aim was to gradually become more like companions to them. After about a year, the people started to trust us and a typical visit pretty much consisted of running a vacuum cleaner for five minutes—and talking for half an hour!"

Michelle adds that she and other S.H.O.P. members formed close friendships with the seniors. "I keep in touch with some of my people, writing to them and stopping by for visits when I'm home on school breaks." She points out that S.H.O.P. volunteers take special care to follow through on their commitments to the people they visit. "Several years ago, a teacher at our local elementary school wrote to the group and asked if we could visit her mother and father," Michelle recalls. "She explained that her dad had been the best father in the neighborhood—doing a lot for local kids, playing Santa Claus for them at Christmas, things like that.

"But then he got sick (he had leukemia), and he'd been confined to the house for a couple of years. He wouldn't leave his bedroom or get dressed. Then, when he heard we were coming to visit, he was very excited. He got out of bed, got dressed up, and was sitting in the living room waiting for us to arrive!"

The teens visited this particular man on a regular basis, and when he passed away last year, they realized his wife would need extra help. "She's having a rough time of it. She doesn't have a companion to talk with anymore, so the group is trying to spend a lot of time with her," says Michelle.

When Michelle looks back at the group's beginnings, she's surprised by its success. "At first I didn't think any other students would want to get involved—I thought they wouldn't take the time. I underestimated them. If I could give advice to someone who wants to start a similar organization at his or her school, I'd tell them, 'Don't underestimate your classmates. They'll surprise you by their desire to become involved.' "

Would you like to start a group like S.H.O.P. at your school? Start by recruiting five (or more!) friends, then "advertise" your services through church or temple newsletters, on the bulletin boards at local senior centers, the "Y," and grocery stores.

If you'd like to work with senior citizens on an individual basis, volunteer at a nursing or retirement home, senior center, adult day-care facility, or a meals-on-wheels program that delivers food to shut-ins. Also, check with the local animal shelters, the Humane Society, or the A.S.P.C.A. to find out if one of these organizations sponsors a "pets and people" program (where volunteers transport animals to senior centers and nursing homes for "visits").

One Town's Good Samaritan

DAVID COX

David Cox, of Gallup, New Mexico, has been paralyzed since birth on the left side of his body—but he's never let his disability interfere with his life, or stop him from helping others.

David, who doesn't use a wheelchair to get around ("I just kind of limp along," he says, chuckling), is "on call" for the dozens of elderly residents in his neighborhood. Now 21, David started lending a helping hand when he was 12. "A neighbor phoned one day and asked if I had time to run down to the store and pick up a *TV Guide*," David recalls. "After that, more people began calling to see if I could get them a newspaper or magazine."

During the past 10 years, David has devoted himself to assisting others in numerous ways. "Basically, I help folks with anything they need. I run errands, do their shopping, or take them shopping if they need a lot of things (I want to make sure they get *exactly* what they need!), do repairs around their houses, pull their trash cans out for garbage pickup, and drive people to doctors' appointments." Often, David stops by a senior's home "just to keep them company."

David offers his services for free, though he adds that people often try to pay him. "I've learned that sometimes I've got to accept a little money, because people can get kind of upset if I refuse it. But I don't like to take their money. I just like to help out."

Now a sportscaster at a local radio station, David admits that school activities and time with friends often took a backseat to his work with "my people." "In high school, I was asked to manage the baseball team. I added up all the hours that would be required for practice and games and realized I just couldn't spend that much time on baseball. I couldn't leave *the people* hanging—somebody might need me to do something important for them and I wouldn't be available." So he turned down the managership. "I don't think I missed out on anything, though," says David. "Baseball wasn't my number-one priority. The people were."

That kind of commitment to the townspeople who rely on him is a central part of David's life today. When he goes out of town for a few days ("to see my best friend in Phoenix, for example"), he makes sure his mother and grandmother will look after his charges. "I always make provisions for the people if I'm going to be away," he says, adding that he's become close friends with a number of the town's elderly citizens over the years. "There's one man who's had several strokes. He can't talk, but I've known him for so long I can tell by the look on his face, or the way he moves his head, what he's trying to tell me, what he needs," explains David. "We 'talk.' We just don't have to use regular language."

Would you like to become a "good Samaritan" to the elderly (or ill or disabled) people in your town? Volunteer to mow a

David Cox.

senior citizen's lawn, or shovel a snow-packed sidewalk. Or ask if he'd like you to pick up "something from the store" the next time you go into town or to the mall. By offering to help out in some small way, you'll win that person's trust, and he won't be embarrassed to ask for your assistance.

To find out *which* elderly (or infirm) people in your area need help, check with the clergy at your church or temple.

For more info about programs that pair kids and teen volunteers with the elderly, contact these organizations: American Association of Retired Persons, 1909 K Street, N.W., Washington, D.C. 20049, 202-662-4895; National Council on the Aging, 600 Maryland Avenue, S.W., West Wing 100, Washington, D.C. 20024, 202-479-1200.

PART FOUR

Risking Their Lives
for Others

Scott Stoppard

Pil Lunn

Shawn Bates

Quick Action Saves a Child

SCOTT STOPPARD

November 21, 1989, started out just like any other school day for Scott Stoppard, of Hanover, Ontario. But, that afternoon, an ordinary day quickly turned into a potentially tragic one when Scott saw his four-year-old neighbor, Nathan Robertson, dart into the street in front of an oncoming car.

"I walked Nathan and another little kid home from our bus stop everyday," says Scott, then 14. "The other kid fell down, and when I went to help him up, Nathan must have seen his mom, who was standing across the street from us. When I turned around, I saw Nathan starting to run out into the street.

"My only thought was to get to Nathan before the car did," says Scott, who shot off after the boy and grabbed him, wrapping his arms around the child's head. The car skidded to a stop—but not before it had hit both boys, finally coming to a rest against Scott's arm. (Later, observers would note that Nathan's skull might have been crushed if Scott's arm hadn't protected the child's head.)

"A little girl saw the accident and ran into a nearby house to call an ambulance," Scott recalls. Scott and Nathan were hospi-

Scott Stoppard.

talized, but Nathan was released after a one-day stay. Scott suffered lacerations on his back, bruises, and a hairline fracture and cerebral concussion and stayed at the hospital for a week, then spent two more weeks recuperating at home.

In 1991, Scott was awarded the prestigious Carnegie Medal, which is given by the Carnegie Hero Fund Commission to "one who, at the risk of his or her own life, saves or attempts to save the life of another person."

Do you know a "local hero"? A kid who's risked his or her life to save someone else's? Report that person's act of courage to your local and city newspapers and radio and TV stations.

Water Rescue!

PIL LUNN

Pil Lunn admits he's not a terrific swimmer—in fact, he can "barely swim at all"! But that didn't stop the Lowell, Massachusetts, boy from jumping into the 20-foot-deep Pawtucket Canal in a daring attempt to rescue his cousin, Peuo Tuy.

It happened on Memorial Day in 1990, when Pil was 13 and his cousin was 11. "I wanted to go fishing *alone,*" says Pil, "but she came along." The boy was just about ready to start fishing when he noticed Peuo walking along the rim of the canal, trying to balance herself. Suddenly, she lost her balance and pitched into the water. "Peuo couldn't swim at all," says Pil. "She was thrashing around and having trouble keeping her head above the water. There wasn't any time to run for help—the only thing I could think to do was to jump in and try to save her."

Pil dived into the canal and struggled to keep Peuo's head out of the water. "It was hard," he recalls, "because she was scared and kept pushing *me* down under." As Pil tried to pull the frantic girl toward the canal wall, a man walking down the embankment spotted the two. Larry Schwartz, from Wellesley,

Massachusetts, dived into the water and pulled Pil and Peuo to the brick wall, where he hung onto the cracks with his fingers until rescuers arrived and, using a hook and rope, pulled all three out of the water.

Both Schwartz and Pil Lunn received the Massachusetts Humane Society Award and the Carnegie Hero Fund Commission Award for bravery.

Do you know someone (19 or younger) who's saved another person's life? Or rescued an injured or abandoned animal? Or contributed to their school or community through outstanding volunteer work? We'd like to hear about them! Tell us about your hero or heroine in 250 words or less; be sure to include that person's name, age, address, and phone number (don't forget the area code). Give us *your* phone number, too. Send your "Young Heroes" nominations to: MasterMedia Publishing, 17 East 89th Street, Suite 7D, New York, NY 10128.

He Risked His Life
for His Friends

SHAWN BATES

When fire raced through a one-story wooden Alabama boardinghouse in September 1990, 16-year-old Shawn Bates had only one thought: to save as many of the elderly and infirm residents as possible.

The Greenpond, Alabama, boy, now 18, was staying at the boardinghouse, which was operated by his mother. "I was asleep when the fire alarm went off and woke me," Shawn remembers. "I opened my bedroom door and saw flames reflected against the wall." The teen ran from his room into the home's living room, where he found an elderly man sitting on a couch that was engulfed in flames. "I picked him up and carried him to the middle of a hallway where the fire hadn't gotten to yet," says Shawn. "Then I went back through the living room and into another man's room. The fire had burned through the wall into his room and the headboard of his bed was in flames. I carried him out to the hallway where the first man was."

Shawn then carried the two men and eight more people out of the house. "I just kept going back in to get people," he says.

Despite Shawn's heroic efforts to reach them, four people died in the blaze. "The flames were just too great for me to get to the back of the boardinghouse, where those people were," says Shawn, who was also overcome by smoke inhalation.

Though he's received numerous awards, including the prestigious Carnegie Medal for bravery, Shawn plays down his "hero" status. "I'd grown up knowing most of the people in the house," he says. "They were good friends of mine and I just wanted to help them." Shawn adds, "If anybody ever finds themselves in a position like the one I was in, or anything similar, they should tell themselves not to give up. There's always a chance that you may make a difference in a lot of people's lives.

"I wish I could have saved everybody, but I just thank God that I was able to give the people I *did* get out a little more time to stay in this world. I thank God for helping me through it, too."

Do you know a kid—or adult—who's risked his or her life to save someone else's? Nominate that person for the Carnegie Hero Award! For information, write to: Carnegie Hero Fund Commission, Oliver Building, Suite 2307, 535 Smithfield Street, Pittsburgh, PA 15222-2394, or call 1-800-447-8900.

Caring for Sick Kids, Campaigning for World Health

Ryan White

Patrick Long

Yana Yanovsky

Joey DiPaolo

The Triumph—and Legacy

RYAN WHITE

His name is a household word, and his life was truly a "profile in courage."

Ryan White was the kid from Kokomo, the boy who at 12 contracted AIDS (acquired immune deficiency syndrome) through tainted blood products he had received to treat his hemophilia (an inherited blood disorder). He was the teen who fought—and won—a very public battle against a school district that refused to allow him to attend classes, then went on to become one of the most important and effective spokespersons in the fight against AIDS, and the need to educate people (kids and grownups alike) about AIDS issues.

When the people in his hometown of Kokomo, Indiana, learned that 13-year-old Ryan had AIDS, they mounted a campaign to keep him out of school. With the support of his mother, Jeanne, and his sister, Andrea, Ryan went to court to sue for the right to attend school. During the next three and a half years, almost every newspaper in the country chronicled his legal battle in headline stories, and for Ryan and his family, those were lonely, fear-filled years. Kids in the community called Ryan names, and they often backed away from him, fearing they might "catch" AIDS just by being near the boy. Someone threw eggs at the Whites' family car and slashed its tires. Another person fired a bullet through the family's living room window. Ryan had no real friends, and his sister and mother were virtually ostracized as well.

In 1986, Ryan won his court case—and the right to attend school in Kokomo. But despite this major victory, the Whites knew they couldn't stay in Kokomo; they were still targets of fear, hatred, and prejudice. The family moved to a nearby Indiana town, Cicero, and finally they began to live a somewhat "normal" life.

A few weeks after the Whites arrived in Cicero, one of their young neighbors, 16-year-old Wendy Baker, appeared at the front door. She'd read all the stories about Ryan. She was aware of the nightmare he and his family had endured in Kokomo. She thought he was incredibly brave—and she wanted to welcome him and his family to the community.

Soon, Ryan made *other* friends, and when he started high school in Cicero, he was greeted not with fear, but with acceptance. Aware of what had happened to the Whites in Kokomo, the principal at Ryan's new school took steps to see that Ryan's experience in Cicero would be entirely different. Before Ryan started classes, the school held AIDS seminars for the students and teachers, and sent literature about AIDS to the students' parents. As a result, the school—and community—reacted with compassion and friendship.

When Ryan first moved to Cicero, he was at one of his lowest points, both physically and emotionally. He was nauseated and vomited constantly. His weight had plummeted to 54 pounds. His doctors had given him only a few months to live. But his condition improved dramatically as he and his family settled

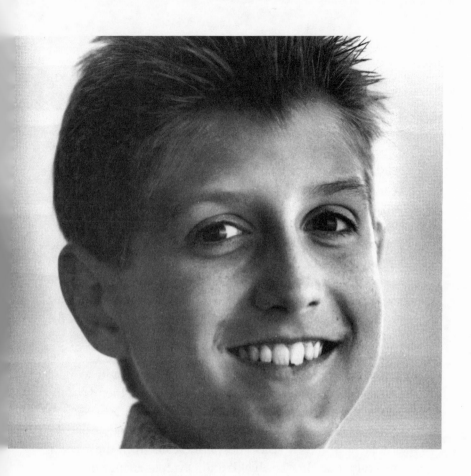

Ryan White.

into their new life, their new home. He made friends quickly and was accepted by almost all of the students at his new school.

Ryan was also becoming a national celebrity, and he appeared on numerous TV talk shows and was the subject of TV docudramas and programs about AIDS. He was also the subject of a prime-time "made for TV" movie, *The Ryan White Story*, which was seen by millions of people.

Whether he was talking with kids at schools, or appearing on TV shows, Ryan was certain of his "mission." He wanted to share the truth about AIDS with others, to dispel the myths, to help people overcome their fears about the disease. And he wanted others to realize that AIDS isn't a "punishment" against any one group of people. It's just a disease that can strike almost anyone, regardless of age, race, or sexual preference.

Dozens of movie and television stars joined Ryan in his crusade to make people more aware of AIDS, and to raise funds for AIDS research. And they became close friends of the teen's at the same time. People like Elton John and Michael Jackson were regular visitors at the boy's home. But despite the fact that he received visits and phone calls from the likes of Tom Cruise and Brooke Shields and Olympic diving champion Greg Louganis, Ryan was a pretty down-to-earth kid, according to his high school friends, and he just wanted to be one of the group.

But, in reality, Ryan White wasn't like all the other kids. He had an incurable illness; he knew from the start that his death could come at any time, and he was prepared for it. He even visited the cemetery in Cicero and he liked it. He felt it was "quiet, peaceful."

On April 8, 1990, 18-year-old Ryan White lost his long battle against AIDS, and the nation—the world—mourned his death. No one will forget Ryan and what he gave to the world. A somewhat shy kid who didn't much like being in the limelight, Ryan was, perhaps more than anyone else, responsible for making a nation aware of the need for AIDS education and the necessity of raising funds so researchers can find a cure for the disease. And he made us stop and realize that PWAs— people with AIDS—deserve compassion, understanding, and respect—and the opportunity to live their lives with dignity.

Would you like to know more about Ryan and his inspiring story? Check out the fine book *Ryan White: My Own Story,* by Ryan White and Ann Marie Cunningham (Dial Books).

To learn more about AIDS (and to find out what *you* can do to help in the search for a cure or to promote AIDS-prevention education), contact these organizations: the Ryan White Foundation, 1-800-444-RYAN; the National AIDS Information Clearinghouse, P.O. Box 6003, Department G, Rockville, MD 20850, 1-800-458-5231; AmFAR (American Foundation for AIDS Research), 733 Third Avenue, 12th Floor, New York, NY 10017, 212-682-7440.

Counseling Kids with Cancer

PATRICK LONG

At four, Patrick Long decided to become a doctor—and the Bellevue, Washington, boy spent countless hours building hospitals and operating rooms with his Lego blocks. When he was 12, Patrick's fantasy hospital became a reality: he was diagnosed with acute lymphocytic leukemia, and he spent the next three and a half years in and out of hospitals, undergoing a series of treatments that would stop his cancer from progressing.

"Those years were a mix of in-patient and out-patient treatment," says Patrick, now 20 and a premed student at Evergreen State College, in Olympia. "At first, I had 24-hour chemotherapy treatments—pretty intensive," he recalls. That was the first stage of therapy. "After that, I'd be on oral medication for a month, then go back into the hospital for five days (for intravenous treatment), then I'd be an out-patient (at the hospital clinic) for two weeks, and after that, I'd go back into the hospital for more aggressive treatment."

Though he missed a lot of school, Patrick managed to graduate with his class ("Just barely!" he says). He also managed to spend many hours offering counsel and comfort to other young cancer patients.

"It started when I was in the hospital," he explains. "A doctor or nurse or social worker would say, 'There's a new patient— would you be willing to talk with him?' I loved to! As a patient, I knew you could get a lot of information from doctors and nurses, but when you're first diagnosed, you're *overwhelmed* with information—and most of it is heavily laden with medical terms. It helps if you can get some of the information from somebody who's not only going through what you are, but is the same age as you.

"I never 'told' the kids anything," says Patrick. "Mainly, I asked questions or let them ask me questions. They wanted to know what a certain medical procedure or treatment would feel like, if it would hurt, or if they'd lose their hair during chemo. I was always honest. *I* required that of my doctors— to let me know exactly what was going on, what they were doing during a certain procedure and why. I didn't want any secrets. That's the approach I took with the other kids, and I think they appreciated it."

During the past few years, Patrick has focused his attention on the American Cancer Society's Camp Good Times (located on Vashon Island, in Washington State). "Good Times is a summer program for kids with almost every form of cancer, from brain tumors to leukemias," says Patrick, who adds that the children's siblings also attend the camp. "Basically, our philosophy and goal is to provide a normal camp situation and experience for the kids. The only limits we put on them are what *they* tell us to. If somebody says, 'I'm too tired to go on this hike,' we say, 'Okay.' The kids are boss."

Patrick, who was himself a camper at Good Times, served as a counselor-in-training for two years, a relief counselor for one,

Patrick Long.

a full-time counselor for another, and is now waterfront director. Several of the counselors are doctors, nurses, and medical students, and the camp also has an official medical team comprised of one doctor and three nurses.

Patrick notes that attending the camp for the first time can be pretty overwhelming. "The first year I went, my mom cried. It was rough. You're going through chemotherapy and you've become very dependent on your own doctors and the hospital. Suddenly, you're taken away from all that and it's a shock." Patrick adds that both the young cancer patients—*and* their siblings—experience homesickness, and the counselors must help *all* the kids deal with their feelings. But he emphasizes that the camp experience is well worth the effort of campers and counselors alike. The children love the camp and take part in a variety of regular camp activities, including swimming, canoeing, biking, hiking, skits, and campfires.

Over the years, the children Patrick has counseled have confronted him with questions most adults wouldn't be able to handle. They often express their fear of dying, and Patrick says, "That's always been a real tough question for me—having a kid ask, 'Am I going to die?' This past summer, one of the campers was an eight-year-old girl who had a brain tumor. About a week after camp ended, her condition started to deteriorate, and I went to her home to visit. She knew she was going to die. There was no doubt about it. She started to talk about death, and the question I remember most clearly was 'Am I going to see Jesus?' That's the toughest question I've ever been faced with. I said, 'Yeah.' The last thing she said to me—and at this point she could barely talk—was 'I love you.' She died four days later.

"Every time someone I've talked with has died, it's been incredibly hard. Not only because someone so young has died, but because that person could have been *me*. It's a little disheartening sometimes, a little scary. But, on the other hand, it also makes me realize how happy I am to be here."

Patrick plans to continue his work with kids, and he hopes, one day, to become a physician who treats children who have cancer. "When I was first diagnosed, I decided I didn't want to be a doctor. I said, 'No way!' I didn't want to have to tell people they might die. My principal doctor kept encouraging me to change my mind, but it wasn't until last year that I decided I had too much to offer *not* to do it. Doctors sometimes say, 'I know how you feel' or 'I know what you mean,' when they really don't know. They've never been through a spinal tap or a 'bone marrow.' I have. I know what it's like to be on the other side, I know how a patient, a little kid who's scared, would like to be treated.

"Right now, I'm thinking of going into pediatric hematology/oncology [cancers of the blood]," says Patrick. "I think it would be cool to work alongside the same doctors who saved *my* life."

Are you interested in working with children who have cancer, or would you like to participate in fund-raising activities that benefit cancer research? Contact your local branch of the American Cancer Society, or call the national headquarters at 1-800-ACS-2345. The Leukemia Society of America also welcomes volunteers. For info, call 212-573-8484.

"Babies don't have a *choice;* they can't make the decision to be born healthy or *un*healthy," says 16-year-old Yana Yanovsky, of Huntington Beach, California. "But their parents *do* have a choice." And that's why Yana has spent the last few years volunteering for the March of Dimes, an organization committed to preventing birth defects.

"It started when I was in eighth grade," she recalls. "Our junior high was a big fund raiser for March of Dimes Walk America, and my principal encouraged me to get involved. I started recruiting walkers for the school, and we came out number one in the area."

When Yana entered high school, she discovered that March of Dimes sponsors a youth council called "Chain Reaction." "I applied, was interviewed, and made it onto the Orange County, California, branch of the council," says Yana, who has served in a variety of capacities—from secretary-treasurer to her present position as chairwoman.

"As chairwoman of the council, I work closely with the other 17 council members and oversee everything our chapter of

Yana Yanovsky.

Chain Reaction does," says Yana. "We have three major goals: (1) To educate young people about things like AIDS, drugs, alcoholism, and teen pregnancy—the emphasis is on how substance abuse and improper prenatal care can cause birth defects, and how the AIDS virus can be passed from mother to child. We provide information about prenatal care, and ways to ensure having a healthy baby for those kids who do get pregnant. (2) To raise money for March of Dimes, and (3) to get more kids involved in the organization and help them develop leadership and communication skills."

While Chain Reaction receives a small amount of money from March of Dimes, the volunteers rely on fund raisers to support their activities. "We hold car rallies, which are like treasure hunts," says Yana. "You get four or five kids in a car, give them a list of clues, and they drive to all the places listed. Last year we raised $600 working at a dog show at a nearby hotel. For three days, we took shifts and cleaned up after the dogs. Actually, it was a lot of fun. We had our own rooms so we got to stay over." Yana adds that council members and other volunteers also get together socially and "just hang out."

An annual health conference is one of the biggest projects sponsored by the Orange County Chain Reaction. "We invite 200 students from area high schools and ask each of them to bring eight kids (they choose those they feel are at risk for AIDS, drug abuse, alcoholism, teen pregnancy, etc.). The conference lasts an entire day and takes place at a hotel.

"We arrange for experts to speak on a variety of topics. This year's theme is 'The Power of Choice,' and we've scheduled people to talk about STDs [sexually transmitted diseases], date rape, drug abuse, and AIDS. Everyone attends the conference for free, and we provide lunch," says Yana.

Yana spends between seven and eight hours a week working on Chain Reaction projects, and she notes that "there is really no time when I actually *see* that I'm making a difference. But when I go to the neonatal units at hospitals and see the babies with birth defects, like those who have holes in their hearts, or low-birth-weight infants, or babies with AIDS, I realize the time I spend working for March of Dimes is worth it. When I hold these babies, I understand how much *still* needs to be done to prevent birth defects—and to give babies a chance at a healthy life.

"A lot of people ask me, 'Why do you do this type of work?' My response is always the same. I say, 'If I *didn't* do it, you'd ask me, 'Why *aren't* you helping?' "

If you would like to become a March of Dimes volunteer, or want to learn more about Chain Reaction, contact the March of Dimes chapter in your area, or write or call the national office: March of Dimes, 1275 Mamaroneck Avenue, White Plains, New York 10605, 914-428-7100.

Joey's Message: "Kids Get AIDS, Too!"

JOEY DIPAOLO

When Joey DiPaolo, of Brooklyn, New York, was four, he underwent open-heart surgery to repair a congenital heart valve defect. During surgery, he received a blood transfusion. Immediately after the operation, Joey's doctors and his parents knew something wasn't right; for several weeks, he ran a high fever, and eight weeks after his discharge from the hospital, Joey developed a severe case of salmonella poisoning and was hospitalized again.

One year after the surgery, a blood test showed that Joey had *another* problem: his blood platelet count was dangerously low (platelets help the blood clot properly, preventing internal hemorrhaging). Joey's doctors feared he had leukemia, but after doing a bone marrow aspiration and more blood tests, they ruled out that disease. Finally, they decided Joey had a condition called idiopathic thrombocytopenia purpura (ITP), in which the blood isn't able to clot the way it should, and they started him on treatments that would remedy the problem. When the treatments didn't work, Joey's doctors recommended that his spleen be removed (removal of the spleen can help stop the destruction of platelets), and Joey underwent surgery in 1987.

"For two years after that—from June of '87 until May of '88—we thought we were a 'normal family,' " says Joey's mother, Carol. "Joey and his little sister, Lauren, both started piano lessons, and Joey joined a bowling league and learned to ride a bike."

Then, in the spring of 1988, all the symptoms of ITP returned. "It was as if Joey had never had his spleen removed," says Carol. "He had bloody noses again, and he got a rash of little red dots [mini-hemorrhages under the skin] all over his body." Tests confirmed that Joey's platelet count had dipped dramatically, and his doctors sent him to a hematologist (a blood specialist). During her examination of Joey, the hematologist noticed that the boy's glands were very swollen. She took Joey's mom and dad aside and said, "Because Joey had a transfusion in 1984—and that was a year when much of the blood supply was tainted with the HIV virus—I'd like to give Joey an HIV antibody test. If it comes back positive, then Joey won't have too long to live. If it comes back negative, you can rule out AIDS and never worry about it again."

Three weeks later, the doctor called the DiPaolos with the test results: Joey was HIV positive. He was infected with human immunodeficiency virus, the virus that causes AIDS. "We got the news on June 21, Joey's father's birthday—and the first day of summer," says Carol. "It was a terrible 'birthday present' for Joey's dad.

"*My* whole world crashed in around me," adds Carol. "I started to grieve for my son, as if he'd already died."

The DiPaolos decided not to tell Joey he was HIV positive. "We thought if he knew, he'd give up and die on us," says his mother. "And his father and I weren't dealing well with the

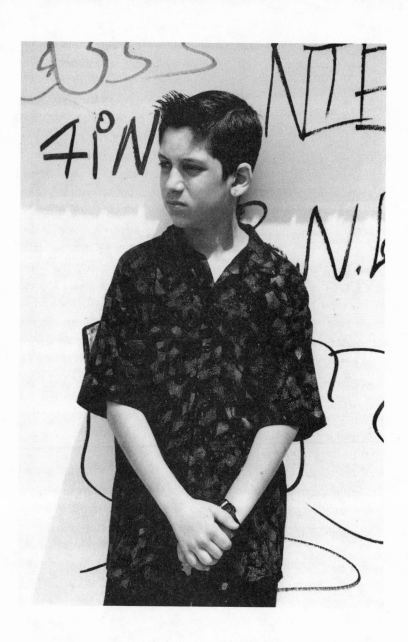

Joey DiPaolo.

situation. We were protecting ourselves by not telling him. We felt that as long as we didn't tell him about his illness, in a way it didn't exist."

Ironically, Joey knew, almost from the day the test results came back, that he was HIV positive, but he decided against telling his parents he knew because he wanted to protect *them.* Seven months after the diagnosis, Joey started treatments with the drug DDI at the National Cancer Institute, in Bethesda, Maryland. At the same time, Carol joined a support group at the center, made up of parents with kids who have AIDS or are HIV positive. "At that first meeting, I told the group my husband and I had decided not to tell Joey he was infected, then I recited all our reasons," says Carol. "Several of the parents looked at me in astonishment and one said, 'He doesn't *know?* That's strange. He's outside in the waiting room, talking with our children and asking, "Do you have cancer or HIV?" If one of the kids says, "I have HIV," Joey says, "Yeah, me too!" ' "

When Joey's mom asked how he'd found out, he explained that whenever his doctors asked him to leave the room so they could talk with his parents in private, he'd pressed his ear up against the door and listened! Joey was well aware that he had a virus called HIV and that it caused AIDS, but he didn't know the full implications of the disease or that, as yet, there was no cure. "I didn't want to upset you," he told his mom. He knew she'd been taking the news of his diagnosis "really hard."

At that point, Carol and Joey sat down and discussed all the issues surrounding AIDS. "I told Joey not to tell *anyone,* not even his best friends, he was HIV positive," recalls Carol. "We knew how people might react, that they might reject Joey, or that we could be run out of town like Ryan White and his family, or have our house burned down like the Ray family [the Rays, of Florida, have several children who are infected with the AIDS virus]."

In February of 1990, Joey came down with bacterial pneumonia, and was hospitalized. Very quickly, the bacteria seeped into his bloodstream and he went into septic shock. One of Joey's kidneys shut down, he had internal bleeding, and his temperature shot up to 106 degrees. "Joey's blood pressure was 'zip,' " says Carol. In order for blood to reach his most important organs—the brain and heart—Joey was positioned so that his head almost touched the floor and his arms and legs were elevated. "In that position, with little or no blood flow to the extremities, Joey could have lost both his arms and legs," says Carol. "To this day, the doctors are surprised that he didn't have to have his limbs amputated." Joey's doctors gave him 48 hours at most. "They told me to go out and start arranging for the funeral," says Carol. "But he fought so hard to live. He survived—and without any scars." (In addition to the possibility of amputation, Joey ran the risk of suffering brain damage because of a lack of blood flow—and oxygen—to his brain.)

"I don't remember anything about those two days," says Joey, who was semiconscious throughout the ordeal. "It was a total waste of two days in my life!"

When he came home from the hospital, Joey continued to keep "the secret." He told his friends he was suffering from a recurrence of ITP, but he didn't like all the secrecy. He *wanted* to tell his friends about his condition, but he was afraid he'd lose them.

That June, while watching the local news, Joey caught an update on the Seventh International AIDS Conference, which was taking place in San Francisco. He called to his mom, who was in the kitchen preparing dinner. "Look at this!" he said. "They're talking about AIDS on TV." Carol replied, "Oh, yeah? What's going on?" "Well," said Joey, "all they're doing is showing a lot of white gay men pushing IV poles around. Where are the *kids* who have AIDS? Why aren't they telling people that children and ladies and *everybody* can get AIDS?" Joey demanded. "No one is ever going to know this until they [the media] start telling the truth!"

Carol agreed and asked Joey what he thought they should do about the situation.

"I think we should go and sit on President Bush's front lawn," he answered.

One month later, the DiPaolo family traveled to California to take part in the Sunburst AIDS Project camp for kids with AIDS. "It was a wonderful, empowering experience," says Carol, who—thanks to Joey's idea about sitting on the President's lawn—proposed that other families attending the camp get together and go to Washington "to make Congress more aware of the need for research in the field of pediatric AIDS." In June of the following year, 300 families gathered in Washington for the first National Children's AIDS Awareness Day, "camping out" in front of the Capitol building.

Soon after the DiPaolos returned from camp, a local AIDS-awareness group, Northern Lights Alternative, asked Joey if he would like to introduce actress Kathleen Turner to the press at a fund-raising dinner in Manhattan. Joey said, "Sure!"

A few days after the event, a small photo of Joey and Turner appeared in the *New York Post,* with a caption that read: "Joey DiPaolo, age seven, introduces Kathleen Turner at a fundraising dinner for AIDS. . . ." The newspaper had gotten Joey's age wrong; he was just about to turn ten.

Soon after the picture appeared, Joey was at his best friend Peter's house, and the two were in Peter's family's swimming pool. "So how're ya doing, seven-year-old?" Peter asked. Instantly, Joey realized Peter and his family had seen the picture in the *Post.*

"I said, 'I have to go home for a minute. I'll be right back,' "

Joey recalls. As Joey was leaving the yard, Peter's parents appeared in the doorway of the house and asked him where he was going. Joey replied that he'd left something at home. Peter's mother said, "Well, I hope you'll come right back."

Joey dashed into his own home and told his mom what had happened. "They know I have HIV and they said to come back."

"That means they want you in their home," said Carol. "Hurry up—go back!" (In the meantime, she gathered together all her literature about AIDS and headed for Peter's home, too. "She knew she was going to have to talk with his parents," explains Joey.)

When Joey returned to Peter's, his friend said, "So, are you going to get in the pool or what?"

"We started talking and stuff," says Joey, "and Peter asked, 'You're going to get better, aren't you?' I said, 'I hope so.'"

The fact that Peter knew about Joey's condition—and still wanted to be his best friend—was a great relief to Joey. He felt he was ready to "go public," and he got his chance very soon.

Shortly before Joey was scheduled to start junior high, Northern Lights Alternative approached the DiPaolos again and asked if they would consent to being interviewed for a *New York Newsday* story about families with children who have AIDS. Joey was all for the interview. "Peter knows now and he doesn't care. I'm glad it's out."

When the *Newsday* reporter came to Joey's house to do the interview, she saw that something extraordinary was going on. "We were working on the National Children's AIDS Awareness Day," explains Carol, "and a volunteer was working on a computer in one room and the phones were ringing off the hooks." Later, the *Newsday* reporter called and said her editor had been very impressed by Joey's story—and by the work he and his family were doing. The paper would like to run Joey's story as a *separate,* full-length feature. Would that be okay? The DiPaolos agreed.

In the meantime, Carol DiPaolo had met with the principal and vice-principal at Joey's new school. "We hadn't told the administration at Joey's elementary school about his HIV status," explains Carol, "but we realized the school and teachers should know—for Joey's sake." At first, the school administration and district superintendent decided to tell only the school nurse—until Carol mentioned the *Newsday* article that was about to break. Very quickly, AIDS-awareness education began in Joey's new school, starting with seminars for the teaching staff.

On Joey's first day at his new school, his picture appeared on the cover of *New York Newsday* with the headline: "Now My School Knows I Have AIDS." (Joey had developed a case of thrush in his esophagus, which meant he was considered to have full-blown AIDS.)

"At first, we thought there wasn't going to be a backlash," says Carol, "since no one from the school called us that first day. We thought, 'This is wonderful; society is finally realizing that people with AIDS can function normally and that they don't pose a threat to others.' Then, on Friday afternoon, we got a call from the principal. Twelve families had demanded that Joey be withdrawn from school." The principal explained that Joey's parents had no intention of withdrawing him. The parents then demanded that their children be transferred out of Joey's classes. The principal explained that this was not possible. Finally, the parents said, "Okay. Then we want him to have his own toilet facilities and drinking fountain, and we want him to eat lunch by himself, not with the other children."

"We were right back in the Ryan White era," says Carol, who

adds that the 12 families planned to gather parents from *other* schools in the district to join in a protest against the principal's decision to allow Joey to remain in school.

The DiPaolos told the principal they had no option other than to alert the media. From that Friday through the following Monday, Joey appeared on every major New York City news show, and on a number of national TV talk shows, including *Good Morning America, Joan Rivers, Donahue,* and *Geraldo.*

"I was a little nervous at first," Joey admits, "but I got the hang of it pretty quickly. I explained that all I wanted to do was go to school, that I wasn't a threat to the other kids—and that people *had* to learn about AIDS." As a result of Joey's courage, the protesters backed down, and today, Joey is not only accepted by his peers at his junior high, but the kids *and* their parents have become educated about AIDS. "At first, a few kids said, 'Oh, AIDS—get away from us!'" Joey notes. "But my friends stood up for me and those kids said, 'Well, if you guys hang out with him, we guess it's okay for us to.'"

In April of 1990, Joey was hospitalized again, this time with chicken pox. "It was then that Ryan White was so ill," Carol remembers, "and Joey was engrossed in the story, watching all the news flashes and updates on Ryan's condition on his hospital TV.

"One day he turned to me and said, 'Mom, if anything happens to Ryan, the message still has to get out there.'"

Joey adds, "When Ryan White died, I knew someone had to take his place. I wanted to finish what he'd started."

And, for the last two years, that's what Joey has done. He's traveled to dozens of schools (from elementary schools to colleges), speaking to kids about AIDS awareness and prevention. "I tell kids if they're going to have sex, to protect themselves, or don't have sex at all. I tell them AIDS can be spread by doing drugs and sharing needles, and I tell them exactly how they can and *can't* get AIDS," says Joey, who also "plays games" with the students. "In one game, I give each kid a piece of paper. Four pieces will have the word 'AIDS' on them. The others will say, 'You don't have AIDS.' They have to go through the whole day, not telling anyone what their paper says. It shows them how hard it is to be forced to keep a secret like that."

In another exercise, Joey asks a student from the audience to come forward, then starts dealing cards (some red, some black) to that person. The student says "stop" at various intervals, and when he does, Joey puts a card into a separate pile. When the student accumulates 10 cards in the "random" pile, he then turns each one over to discover the color. "Every red card represents an HIV-infected person the student supposedly had sex with," explains Joey. "A girl in one class ended up with nine red cards, which meant she could have been infected by nine different people." But Joey goes on to explain that even *one red card*—or having sex with just one person who has HIV—can put you at risk for infection.

In addition to making speeches at schools and various AIDS fund-raising functions, Joey recently appeared in an HBO docudrama *(Blood Brothers: The Joey DiPaolo Story),* based on his life. "I came on before the movie and at the end," says Joey, "and talked about AIDS awareness."

Juggling speaking engagements, public appearances, and medical treatments with school can be tricky, according to Joey. "One month I had a lot of speaking engagements and I also had to go to the National Institutes of Health (in Bethesda, MD) twice for treatments," he says. "I think I went to school three days that month! And when that happens, my teachers say, 'Okay, you're going to be gone for a while, but when you get back, you have to catch up.' "

Being thrust into the limelight at such an early age hasn't been easy for Joey, now 13, but he recognizes that he has a mission to fulfill. He knows he plays an important role in making people more aware of AIDS issues, the facts and the myths—of telling them that AIDS is an "equal opportunity" disease that everyone, including *kids,* can get. And, as Joey's mother says, "He's a fighter," so he's up to the challenge.

Would you like to learn more about AIDS prevention? Or the ways you can—and can't—get AIDS? Or do you want to become involved in projects that raise funds for AIDS research?

Contact: The Ryan White Foundation, 1-800-444-RYAN, or the National AIDS Hotline, 1-800-342-AIDS.

Epilogue

From the Authors . . .

We've introduced you to 26 amazing kids—and we hope their stories have inspired *you* to "make a difference" in your school, or community—or our world. Whether you volunteer at a soup kitchen or join an environmental group or donate your time and services at a nursing home, hospital, or animal shelter, you *are* needed and your efforts *can* make your country, and this earth, a better place for everyone.

Each year, thousands of kids give time, energy, and money to volunteer projects, or risk their lives to save someone else's, and we wish we could have told the stories of each and every person! We'd like to close by recognizing several dozen more outstanding young people who do truly make a difference.

Good Kids to Know

Seven-year-old *Tyler Brickman,* of Okeene, Oklahoma, thinks his mom, Lynn, is pretty special. And out of love for his mother, who has multiple sclerosis, Tyler walked 9.3 miles in the Super Cities Walk for MS last April. Tyler got enough people to sponsor him that he was able to collect $260 in pledges, which will be used to help in the search for a cure for MS.

Jason Jeknavorian, 12, of Chula Vista, California, was just nine when he saved his sister from drowning. Jason's mom, Denise, was bathing nine-month-old Marissa, when she had to leave the bathroom for a minute. She asked Jason to watch Marissa as the water drained from the tub.

Suddenly, Denise heard Jason yelling, "Mommy, help!" When Denise ran back into the bathroom, she found Jason holding Marissa high above the water, as the baby shook violently, then "went stiff." Jason explained that Marissa's head had dropped back into the water, and when he lifted her out of the tub, she'd started to shake. Jason dialed 911, as his mother cradled the baby in her arms. Later, doctors told the Jeknavorians that Marissa had suffered a seizure, and that Jason's fast action had saved his sister's life.

Patrick Duffin, 8, of Bangor, Pennsylvania, believes that "honesty is the best policy." When he recently found $397 in cash on the floor at a wrestling meet, he immediately turned the money over to an adult at the door. As it turned out, the money belonged to a woman who had just cashed her paycheck.

The students (ages 2 through 14) at the *Witness for Christ Christian Day School,* in Indianapolis, Indiana, spend many hours of their free time visiting the elderly at nursing homes throughout the area, singing and reading to the residents.

At *Georgetown University,* in Washington, D.C., hundreds of student volunteers work at a low-income housing project and area shelters, tutoring homeless and needy children.

At *McAlister College,* in St. Paul, Minnesota, students collect, then sell, mittens to fellow students—who then give their purchases to local shelters. The money goes to the shelters, too.

At *Xavier University,* in Cincinnati, 50 students built a cardboard "shantytown" and lived in the boxes for four days, collecting donations from passersby, which they donated to area shelters.

Edwin Santos, 19, of New York City, has spent nine years creating and caring for a community garden on Manhattan's Lower East Side.

Fourteen-year-old *Donny Seher,* of Salt Lake City, was one of the leaders of a class of fifth-graders who alerted the neighborhood to a toxic dump, lobbied the city to have it cleaned up, and then pushed for state legislation to help pay for future cleanups.

Darlene Rodriguez, 18, of Miami, Florida, teaches inner-city kids about environmental issues and has created a bilingual (English/Spanish) series of brochures about environmental action.

Thirteen-year-old *Jeff Lazar,* of Oak Park, Michigan, has worked to raise money for the Muscular Dystrophy Association since he was five. Jeff has organized a carnival that raises several thousand dollars annually for the cause.

When *John DeMarco,* 19, of Philadelphia, was just 13, he took a stand against racism in his community, reporting, and later testifying against, a neighbor who had painted racial slurs on a house a black family was considering buying.

Tanja Vogt, 18, of West Milford, New Jersey, led a campaign to ban Styrofoam from her school cafeteria, then from her hometown, and, later, from fast-food restaurant chains.

After a neighborhood child was struck by a car while playing in the street, 14-year-old *James Ale,* of Davie, Florida, successfully lobbied the city for a playground in his community, so kids would have a safe place to play.

Andrew Holleman, 17, of Chelmsford, Massachusetts, successfully researched and campaigned against a condominium project that threatened to destroy a wetlands area near his home.

Erica Hansen, 12, of Flagstaff, Arizona, supports a foster child by raising $20 a month collecting and recycling bottles, walking dogs, and doing other chores.

Kerri Trusty, 15, of Great Falls, Montana, launched a project called "Kerri's Mittens," when she was 10. Kerri organized a community drive to collect mittens, hats, and socks to give to needy people. She received donations from local businesses and has gotten community support through public service announcements on area radio and TV stations.

Alicia Sims, 19, of Sidell, Louisiana, gives counsel and comfort to kids who've lost a sibling. When Alicia's brother died, she couldn't find a support group that dealt with sibling bereavement. So she started the only New Mexico support group for children (and parents) who are going through the grieving process. Since then, she's toured the country, hosting workshops on the needs of kids who have experienced losses, and has written a book telling about her own loss *(Am I Still a Sister?).*

Dan Weber, 17, of Boise, Idaho, started an Adopt-a-Grandparent Program (as part of an Eagle Scout project), and, along with 20 friends, cared for elderly residents at a local nursing home.

Billy Joe Thomas, 14, of Seattle, Washington, won eight trips to Disneyland for selling the most tickets to local Scout shows. He then gave the trips to kids who have incurable illnesses.

Brooke Schneider, 8, of Yonkers, New York, spends one Saturday a month helping her dad, Cliff, and several other members of St. John's Episcopal Church, in Tuckahoe, New York, cook a meal for the Sharing Community (a Yonkers organization serving the homeless). Brooke has also spent many Thanksgivings and Christmases at the center, setting tables and arranging centerpieces "so the homeless people can have a nice holiday meal, too."

Nine-year-old *Mark Hibbs* is a regular visitor at the Westview Nursing Home, in Center, Missouri. Mark brings the elderly residents crafts projects, and plays games with them (he's even developed a "nursing-home-style" basketball game they can take part in!). For a recent holiday party, Mark made a piñata, filled with goodies, for his elderly friends to break. When the residents at Westview hear that Mark is coming to visit, their faces light up with joy—and for good reason!

When 12-year-old *William Robert*'s mom underwent brain surgery in 1991, the Perry, Kansas, boy became her "quiet, constant source of strength." From the moment he understood what was happening, William "grew up," says his mother, Carolyn. During her one-year recovery, he willingly took over many of the household chores, and never complained when his own activities had to take a "backseat." Says his mother, "Just knowing he was at home allowed me to relax as much as possible." Robert's mom is much better now, and the boy is involved in school activities and enjoying his busy life. "But I know that if I need him, he'll be there for me," says Carolyn.

When the three *Leeper* kids (*Allison,* 8, *Courtney,* 5, and *Aaron,* 1) found a calf that had been abandoned by its mother, they became the little animal's "parents." The Niantic, Illinois, trio attached a nipple to a bucket and nursed the calf

("George") until he was old enough—and strong enough—to eat solid food.

Tyler Alvey was born with a muscle disorder that prevents him from standing erect or walking very far, but his condition didn't stop the Sturgis, Kentucky, boy, who's two and a half, from saving his six-month-old sister, Rachel. Tyler's mom, Kim, had taken the two children out into the yard while she burned scrap paper. A gust of wind picked up a piece of burning paper and blew it into the bordering field of dry grass. Flames quickly soared and as Kim tried to douse the fire, she told Tyler to push baby Rachel's stroller to safety. Rather than crying or hanging onto his mom, Tyler, who can barely walk, calmly pushed the stroller to the other side of the house—far away from the flames. A neighbor, who was driving by, saw what was happening and was able to extinguish the fire.

Nine-year-old *Gail Wubbenhorst,* of Westby, Wisconsin, helped "save" her grandmother's 20-year-plus Avon business. When Irene Wubbenhorst developed severe knee problems, and underwent knee-replacement surgery, she was afraid her days of selling Avon products were over. But Gail stepped in and not only delivered back orders, but also wrote up enough *new* orders to keep her grandmother's sales up to $500 to $600 during each campaign (Gail's grandfather drove the girl to homes she couldn't walk to). Today, Gail rides along with her grandmother on "sales calls." And to the residents of Westby, she's the new Avon representative!

When 16-year-old *Tilmon Peterson,* of Imperial Beach, California, saw a man "dump" a big white dog on a nearby street corner, he knew he had to help the animal. "I didn't recognize the man," says Tilmon. "He must have been passing through, and he was just going to leave the dog there to take care of itself." Tilmon, who was 12 at the time, took the dog home and cared for it until the local A.S.P.C.A. could find a permanent home for the animal ("We couldn't keep him," explains Tilmon, "since we lived in an apartment"). Tilmon has a special reason for helping homeless animals (and people): he and his family once lived in a shelter for the homeless themselves.

Eighteen-year-old *John Thompson,* of Hursfield, North Dakota, had both arms ripped off in a farming accident in 1992. With blood oozing from the stumps of his arms, John ran 400 feet uphill to his house and used the bone that dangled from his left shoulder to pry open the door. Holding a pen in his teeth, he dialed his uncle's phone number, then waited in the bathroom for 30 minutes (so he wouldn't drip blood on his mom's carpet!) until help arrived.

John was airlifted to North Memorial Hospital in Minneapolis, where a team of six microsurgeons successfully reattached both of his arms (John had enough presence of mind to ask the ambulance crew to find the severed limbs and pack them in ice). The boy's courage has been an inspiration to everyone—from the people in his farming community to his doctors to those of us who've read about his experience in newspapers and magazines. Last May, just six months after the accident, John Thompson graduated, with the rest of his class, from high school—something he'd promised himself he'd do, no matter what.

When *Charlie Cunningham* was 9, his family's Christmas tree toppled and caught on fire—and Charlie was engulfed in flames that burned over 65 percent of his body. As firemen carried him from the burning house, Charlie remembers one saying, "Don't rush this one, he'll never make it."

But Charlie did make it—and he spent the next eight years undergoing intensive treatment and rehabilitative therapy at St. Mary's Hospital for Children, in Bayside, New York (this unique hospital cares for chronically or terminally ill kids, and has a school on its grounds). Charlie overcame a great deal during those years—he had three operations to "release" scar tissue; he attended occupational therapy and physical therapy classes and worked hard to exercise daily to loosen up his skin and muscles, which were pulled tight because of the burns; and when he was able to go out in public, he endured the rude stares of unfeeling people who focused on his badly burned face.

But Charlie was a happy-go-lucky kid who loved people—and that's part of what made him decide to become a volunteer at St. Mary's. At 18, Charlie spent many hours at the hospital, helping kids with arts and crafts projects, or in sports activities. He wanted to serve as a "role model" for them, to help other sick or injured kids realize they *can* overcome extreme adversity. Today at 22, Charlie is a child-care technician at St. Mary's, and an important part of the medical team. His dream? To go to medical school and become a doctor—so he can continue to help others.

Five-year-old *Joshua Thomas,* of Kokomo, Indiana, has developed a caring and compassionate nature at an unusually early age. When his grandmother was hospitalized with a terminal illness, Joshua spent many hours at her side. He wasn't afraid of the hospital trappings—the tubes in his grandmother's arms, or the oxygen mask she needed in order to breathe. Each day for the last two weeks of his grandmother's life, Joshua stroked the woman's hair or arm, or touched her face, and said, "Grandma, it's Josh. I'm here for you. I love you." Joshua's concern for others continues, and when he learned that a neighbor had been hospitalized, he begged to be allowed to visit her. He picked a bouquet of flowers, and at the hospital, hopped up onto the woman's bed and started to chat cheerfully with her. By the time Joshua left, the woman was smiling—and looking forward to his next visit.

Danny Bernhardt, 8, of Laguna Niguel, California, is a true friend of the environment—and wildlife. Danny makes certain every member of his family recycles trash—and he's saved quite a few wild animals, including nine orphaned baby opossums and a baby bird ("Bandit"). Danny cares for his young charges until they're able to care for themselves, then he sets them free.

For three years during junior high, *Avan Patel,* 15, sold daffodils to raise money for the American Cancer Society. Avan has always been concerned about helping people who have cancer, and when she graduated from junior high, she wanted to continue her fund-raising efforts. So, every year, the Elmhurst, New York, girl calls her former vice-principal and asks to help out with the school's daffodil sales, raising approximately $350 for the cause.

Laura Koerber, 13, of Akron, Ohio, has always loved animals, and when her beloved dog, Queenie, died, Laura decided to adopt a new pet at the Pet Guards Animal Shelter. Laura was so moved by the plight of the homeless animals, she became a volunteer at the shelter, bathing, grooming, feeding, and exercising the animals, as well as cleaning their cages. Seeing that many of the dogs and cats suffered from severe flea infestation, Laura would devote many hours bathing and grooming them, to make them adoptable. After intensive bathing and brushing, the animals soon had vibrant, lustrous coats—and were ready for adoption by loving families. Thanks to people like Laura, the lives of many of the dogs and cats at Pet Guards have been saved.

Like many students, 8-year-old *Aaron Beil,* of Hinsdall, Montana, has a classmate who is not liked and is picked on, says his mom, Roxanne. Nonetheless, Aaron "has gone out of his way to help her out by buying Girl Scout cookies from her and attending her birthday party"—despite the fact that he was just one of two children there and the only boy besides. "We live in a very rural area, and he has truly learned the meaning of friendship," she says.

In Brighton, Michigan, it's "not unusual" to see *Gretchen VanHeyningen,* 13, "bottle feeding a new litter of kittens or puppies whose mother is ill or has been killed," reports her grandmother, Jean Long. For several years, Gretchen has been active in a "Save the Animals" program, and when her small charges are ready, she finds homes for them, or if they're wild creatures, she releases them into their natural environment. Her most significant action to date? She helped rescue animal victims when a pet store fire broke out! Not surprisingly, Gretchen's life's goal is to become a veterinarian.

Lisa Wisniewski turned 8 last December, and for that birthday, she opted out of a traditional party. Instead of gifts for herself, she asked her guests to bring holiday food for the needy (it was just 10 days till Christmas)—and she ended up with four large boxes to donate to the less-fortunate citizens of Arlington Heights, Illinois.

Even at 7 years of age, love and responsibility are second nature to *Daniel Yeager* of Allison Park, Pennsylvania. Because

Daniel's 11-year-older brother, Matthew, has muscular dystrophy, Daniel acts as Matthew's arms and legs. Without help, Matthew can't move at all, so Daniel assists him in sitting up, getting in and out of his wheelchair, and performing other tasks. Though he can't be at home every second, Daniel's concern for Matthew's well-being is always his top priority.

Early on, *Regina Petruzzi* realized she had a gift—her singing voice—and ever since has used it to bring joy to her community of Cape Coral, Florida. Now 18, Regina began her volunteer singing at age 7 for churches, youth groups, senior citizens in nursing homes, homeless children, the community theater, weddings, fund raisers, and veterans. Recently, she went into Florida prisons and, through inspirational songs, brought a bit of music and hope to many male and female inmates.

Two years ago, *Ashley Wyche,* then 5 years old, sadly watched as her mother—Navy Lieutenant Sabrina Wyche, a nurse—donned camouflage clothing and headed for a tour of duty in Desert Storm. Not knowing if she would ever see her again, Ashley drew a portrait of her mother as she last saw her—and for it won a Portsmouth, Virginia, citywide award for kindergarten through third grade! Happily, Ashley and her mom were reunited after Sabrina spent seven months in the Persian Gulf.

Along with his classmates in Pittsburgh, Pennsylvania, 10-year-old *Andy Jones* had the assignment of selling candy or washing cars to pay for a trip to summer camp. Though Andy reached his goal in just one day, he continued to work hard—and gave his excess money to his less-fortunate friends so that they, too, could attend the camp!

"We don't even know what started it all," says his mother, Gene, of 7-year-old *Charles Burton*. It seems that at age 5, Charles began what he calls his "poor basket." He raised money by doing extra chores and recycling cans and bottles, and gave the money to the Salvation Army to feed the poor. The next year, he offered his proceeds to a Desert Storm widow with four young children, and this year he asked the Mewick, Michigan, Lion's Club to give his charitable contribution to the blind. Every year, Charles gets out his basket in January and works on filling it until May—with no help from his folks.

Bryan Devar, age 9, knows not to play with fire himself but taught the important lesson to a neighbor—the hard way. While visiting the other boy, Bryan was ignited by a gas can dropped by the friend. Though severely burned—45 percent of his body was injured—Bryan put out the fire. Instantly, it flamed up again, and again he put it out; then he called the Blythe, California, emergency 911 and waited for rescue in the front yard. After many skin graft operations, Bryan is slowly recovering.

Last summer, 12-year-old *James Thomas* witnessed a terrible crime in Cincinnati, Ohio. In trying to escape a man bent on stealing her money, a woman jumped in her car to get away. But the man hurled a piece of asphalt through the window, and it smashed into her neck along with the shattered glass. In a state of shock, she got out of her car and began wandering around, bleeding badly. Having seen what happened, James quickly went up to her and helped her back to her office building. The police were called and James accompanied them to the scene of the crime, showed them where the man had fled, and identified the man for the arrest. Later, the man tried three times to scare James out of testifying, by threatening him and his family. After almost a year of postponements and extensions, the trial was held, and James spent two-and-a-half hours on the witness stand, facing the accused "even though he was scared stiff," says the sister of the victim. "Why?" she adds. "Because in the West End, a young black boy does not go against an older black man to help a white woman. James didn't care about race—he just wanted to do what was right—and on May 29 the accused was found guilty, thanks to James Thomas."

Riverside, California, has many reasons to be grateful for the Riverside Ropers 4H Club, which has a continuous fund raiser of selling Avon products, and makes donations to those in need. One recent incident was the tragic death of a man (the son of an Avon representative) who left a widow and small daughter; 4H-er *Jennifer Hunt,* age 13, spearheaded a special fund raiser for the family. In another case, a rural Riverside man lost a leg to cancer and is unable to care for his animals and property. Along with her fellow 4H-ers, 10-year-old *Mary Hunt,* Jennifer's sister, visits his home a half dozen times a year and spends the day doing hard labor, shoveling manure and pushing a wheelbarrow to clean out the barn and tidy up the yard.

Another group that makes a difference includes *Jeff Strickley, Brian Peterson, Jessica Rich,* and *Keith Tyner,* all 15, from Hobart, Indiana. In the summer of 1991, the United Methodist Church youth group traveled to an Appalachian mountain town in Kentucky to help remodel a house for a family that wasn't well off. The demanding daily chores included putting up drywall, outside siding, and windows and doors, and redoing the entire kitchen. Each night for a week, the kids stayed in a local school and slept on the floor. This summer they have another major project scheduled.

At only 3 years of age, *Cameron Scherer* was so afraid of strangers that he wouldn't say a word to his great-grandmother, whom he had seen only twice. When VisaVo ("Great-grandmother" in Portuguese) had a stroke, little Cam was taken to the hospital to visit her and told that she was very sick and needed lots of love to get better. Despite his fears, the shy boy from Willard, Ohio, entered the room, took a cautious look around, and then climbed up on the bed and gave VisaVo a big hug and kiss. From then on, Cam's constant presence—and the special bond brought by kisses and hugs and talk—gave VisaVo the will to work a little harder to recover and return home.

Very few addicts have a fighting chance against crack, and 12-year-old *Atiya Easterling* was devastated four years ago when she saw a favorite uncle in its grip. After talking over the crisis with her parents, she tried to think of something—anything—she could do to help. Her efforts led to a sketch of a crack pipe and the words "Believe the Hype—Put Down the Pipe" (taken from a rap song), which she then had printed on T-shirts. Since that time, more than 5,000 of Atiya's shirts have been sold or given away in her community of Queens, New York, and across the country; just as important, the message reached Atiya's uncle—he is now drug-free, thanks to her compassion and action.

Another soldier in the war against drugs is *Raymond Smith*, 12, of Tucson, Arizona. Ray is his state's leadership representative for the DARE (Drug Abuse Resistance Education) program, and on behalf of 600,000 Arizona children, he recently met in

Washington, D.C., with the 49 other state reps. Back at home, Ray lectures elementary school children on drug abuse, and its effects on the mind and body.

Red Oak, Iowa, has a very special sports complex, thanks to 15-year-old *Jason Hamman.* For his Eagle Scout service project, Jason contacted the Red Oak Trees Forever Committee to see about planting trees at the complex both to beautify and to serve as a windbreak. Next he asked various organizations for financial aid, and altogether raised over $8,000. With those funds, he was able to buy more than 60 types of trees, and, with fellow Scouts and other service groups, saw his dream come true as they were planted at the complex.

Resources

Organizations That Recognize "Local Heroes"

Do you know a kid who's done something really outstanding to help others? Tell these organizations about him or her!

The Giraffe Project
120 Second Street
P.O. Box 759
Langley (Whidbey Island), WA 98260
1-800-344-TALL

The Carnegie Hero Fund Commission
Oliver Building, Suite 2307
535 Smithfield Street
Pittsburgh, PA 15222-2394
1-800-477-8900

Service Groups

Camp Fire
4601 Madison Avenue
Kansas City, MO 64112-1278
816-756-1950
(Or call your area chapter.)

Girl Scouts
830 Third Avenue
New York, NY 10022
1-800-223-0624
(Or call your area chapter.)

Boy Scouts of America
1325 Walnut Hill Lane
Irving, TX 75038-3096
214-580-2000
(Or call your area chapter.)

The Points of Light Foundation
1-800-879-5400
(This organization can link you up with volunteer centers around the country, and provides a booklet on volunteerism.)

United Way of America
701 North Fairfax Street.
Alexandria, VA 22314-2045
703-836-7100
(United Way can match you with the volunteer organization that needs your help and can use your particular talents.)

American Red Cross
17th and D Streets, N.W.
Washington, D.C. 20006
202-737-8300

*Food, Clothes, and Shelter
for the Homeless and Needy*

Food for the Hungry
P.O. Box E
Scottsdale, AZ 85260
1-800-2-HUNGER

Habitat for Humanity
Habitat and Church Streets
Americus, GA 31709
912-924-6935

National Coalition for the Homeless
1621 Connecticut Avenue, N.W.
Suite 400
Washington, D.C. 20009
202-265-2371

USA HARVEST
1-800-872-4366
(Collects and distributes 30 million pounds of food to the homeless in 23 states every year.)

Trevor's Campaign for the Homeless
3415 West Chester Pike
Newtown Square, PA 19073
1-800-TREVORS

The Salvation Army. Call your area branch to find out about volunteer programs and collections for the needy.

Goodwill Industries. Call your local branch for info on volunteer projects and collections for those in need.

Helping the Elderly and Disabled

American Association of Retired Persons (AARP)
1909 K Street, N.W.
Washington, D.C. 20049
202-662-4895

National Council on the Aging
600 Maryland Ave., S.W.
West Wing 100
Washington, D.C. 20024
202-479-1200

Lighthouse for the Blind
800 Second Avenue
New York, NY 10017
212-808-0077
(The Lighthouse needs volunteers to read to people who are visually impaired.)

National Easter Seal Society
2023 West Ogden Avenue
Chicago, IL 60612
312-243-8400
(With 200 chapters around the country, Easter Seals provides many programs that help the disabled. Volunteers are needed for fund-raising projects.)

The National Down Syndrome Society
666 Broadway
New York, NY 10012
1-800-221-4602

Deafness Research Foundation
9 East 38th Street
7th Floor
New York, NY 10016
1-800-535-3323

Substance Abuse and Kids' Protection Groups

National Committee for Prevention of Child Abuse
312-663-3520

The National Crime Prevention Council
202-466-6272

National Runaway Switchboard
312-880-9866

The American Council for Drug Education
301-294-0600

Just Say No Clubs
1-800-258-2766

National Council on Alcoholism
212-206-6770

Kids Against Crime (KAC)
P.O. Box 22004
San Bernardino, CA 92406

Drug-Free Homes/Youthwish, Inc.
27 Eagle Drive
Key Largo, FL 33037

Youth Suicide National Center
415-342-5755

RID (Remove Intoxicated Drivers)
P.O. Box 520
Schenectady, NY 12301

National Coalition to Prevent Impaired Driving
1730 Rhode Island Avenue, N.W.
Suite 600
Washington, D.C. 20036

Working for World Health

American Cancer Society
1-800-ACS-2345

The Leukemia Society of America
600 Third Avenue
4th Floor
New York, NY 10016
212-573-8484

March of Dimes
1275 Mamaroneck Avenue
White Plains, NY 10605
914-428-7100
(March of Dimes works to prevent birth defects; call or write the national headquarters—or your area branch—to find out about volunteer projects.)

National Multiple Sclerosis Society
205 East 42nd Street
New York, NY 10017
212-986-3240
(With 140 chapters throughout the United States, this organization needs volunteers for walk-a-thons and other fund-raising projects.)

The Ryan White Foundation (for information about AIDS)
1-800-444-RYAN

The National AIDS Information Clearinghouse
P.O. Box 6003
Deptartment G
Rockville, MD 20850
1-800-458-5231

AmFAR (American Foundation for AIDS Research)
733 Third Avenue
12th Floor
New York, NY 10017
212-682-7440

AIDS Hotline
1-800-342-AIDS

Cleaning Up (and Saving) the Environment

American Forestry Association
1-800-368-5748

Greenpeace USA
1436 U Street, N.W.
Washington, D.C. 20036
202-466-2823

National Audubon Society
950 Third Avenue
New York, NY 10022
212-832-3200

National Recycling Coalition
1101 30th Street, N.W.
Suite 305
Washington, D.C. 20007
202-625-6406

The Sierra Club
730 Polk Street
San Francisco, CA 94109
415-776-2211

CAPE (Children's Alliance for Protection of the
Environment)
P.O. Box 307
Austin, TX 78767
512-476-2273

Kids Network
National Geographic Society
Educational Services
Department 1001
Washington, D.C. 20077
1-800-368-2728

R.A.I.N. (Rainforest Awareness Information Network)
18802 185th Avenue, N.E.
Woodinville, WA 98072

Check out these "earth-friendly" books and magazines at your
library:
50 Simple Things You Can Do to Save the Earth and *Kid
Heroes of the Environment,* both by EarthWorks Group, Earth-
Works Press.
Natural History Magazine, Ranger Rick Magazine (for younger
kids).

Helping Animals, Protecting Endangered Species

Adopt a Species and Its Habitat
National Wildlife Federation
Department AS
8925 Leesburg Pike
Vienna, VA 22184

Save the Manatee Club
500 North Maitland Avenue
Maitland, FL 32751
1-800-432-JOIN

National Audubon Society
950 Third Avenue
New York, NY 10022
212-832-3200

A.S.P.C.A. (American Society for the Prevention of Cruelty to Animals). Call your local branch, or the national headquarters at 212-876-7700.

The Humane Society of the United States. Call your area chapter, or the national headquarters at 202-452-1100.

Books and magazines to check out:
Secrets of a Wildlife Watcher: A Beginner's Field Guide, by Jim Arnosky (Beech Tree Books).
Wildlife Conservation Magazine, Ranger Rick (for younger children).

About the Authors

JOYCE M. ROCHE oversees strategic marketing and design for Avon Products, Inc. She was selected by *Dollars & Sense* magazine as one of the "top 100 black business and professional women in America," and in 1989 she was identified as one of the "top women to watch in corporate America" by *Business Month* magazine. She lives in New York City and is on the board of directors of the New York Urban League and the corporate advisory board of Queens College.

MARIE RODRIGUEZ is a division sales manager of Avon Products, Inc. She is active in Sister Cities International and her church. She lives with her husband and son in Miami, Florida.

PHYLLIS SCHNEIDER is a former editor-in-chief of *YM* magazine and a former fiction and teen features editor of *Seventeen*.

Additional copies of *Kids Who Make a Difference* may be ordered by sending a check for $8.95 (please add the following for postage and handling: $2.00 for the first copy, $1.00 for each added copy) to:

MasterMedia Limited
17 East 89th Street
New York, NY 10128
212-260-5600
800-334-8232
212-546-7607 (fax)

The authors are available for speeches. Please contact MasterMedias' Speakers' Bureau for availability and fee arrangements. Call Tony Colao at 908-359-1612; fax: 908-359-1647.

Other MasterMedia Books

THE PREGNANCY AND MOTHERHOOD DIARY: Planning the First Year of Your Second Career, by Susan Schiffer Stautberg, is the first and only undated appointment diary that shows how to manage pregnancy and career. ($12.95 spiralbound)

CITIES OF OPPORTUNITY: Finding the Best Place to Work, Live and Prosper in the 1990's and Beyond, by Dr. John Tepper Marlin, explores the job and living options for the next decade and into the next century. This consumer guide and handbook, written by one of the world's experts on cities, selects and features forty-six American cities and metropolitan areas. ($13.95 paper and $24.95 cloth)

THE DOLLARS AND SENSE OF DIVORCE, by Dr. Judith Briles, is the first book to combine practical tips on overcoming the legal hurdles with planning finances before, during, and after divorce. ($10.95 paper)

OUT THE ORGANIZATION: New Career Opportunities for the 1990s, by Robert and Madeleine Swain, is written for the millions of Americans whose jobs are no longer safe, whose companies are not loyal, and who face futures of uncertainty. It gives advice on finding a new job or starting your own business. ($12.95 paper)

AGING PARENTS AND YOU: A Complete Handbook to Help You Help Your Elders Maintain a Healthy, Productive and Independent Life, by Eugenia Anderson-Ellis, is a complete guide to providing care to aging relatives. It gives practical advice and resources to the adults who are helping their elders lead productive and independent lives. ($9.95 paper)

CRITICISM IN YOUR LIFE: How to Give It, How to Take It, How to Make It Work for You, by Dr. Deborah Bright, offers practical advice, in an upbeat, readable, and realistic fashion, for turning criticism into control. Charts and diagrams guide the reader into managing criticism from bosses, spouses, relationships, children, friends, neighbors, and in-laws. ($17.95 cloth)

BEYOND SUCCESS: How Volunteer Service Can Help You Begin Making a Life Instead of Just a Living, by John F. Raynolds III and Eleanor Raynolds, C.B.E., is a unique how-to book targeted to business and professional people considering volunteer work, senior citizens who wish to fill leisure time meaningfully, and students trying out various career options. The book is filled with interviews with celebrities, CEOs, and average citizens who talk about the benefits of service work. ($19.95 cloth)

MANAGING IT ALL: Time-Saving Ideas for Career, Family, Relationships, and Self, by Beverly Benz Treuille and Susan Schiffer Stautberg, is written for women who are juggling careers and families. Over two hundred career women (ranging from a TV anchorwoman to an investment banker) were interviewed. The book contains many humorous anecdotes on saving time and improving the quality of life for self and family. ($9.95 paper)

YOUR HEALTHY BODY, YOUR HEALTHY LIFE: How to Take Control of Your Medical Destiny, by Donald B. Louria, M.D., provides precise advice and strategies that will help you to live a long and healthy life. Learn also about nutrition, exercise, vitamins, and medication, as well as how to control risk factors for major diseases. ($12.95 paper)

THE CONFIDENCE FACTOR: How Self-Esteem Can Change Your Life, by Judith Briles, is based on a nationwide survey of six thousand men and women. Briles explores why women so often feel a lack of self-confidence and have a poor opinion of themselves. She offers step-by-step advice on becoming the person you want to be. ($9.95 paper, $18.95 cloth)

THE SOLUTION TO POLLUTION: 101 Things You Can Do to Clean Up Your Environment, by Laurence Sombke, offers step-by-step techniques on how to conserve more energy, start a recycling center, choose biodegradable products, and proceed with individual environmental cleanup projects. ($7.95 paper)

TAKING CONTROL OF YOUR LIFE: The Secrets of Successful Enterprising Women, by Gail Blanke and Kathleen Walas, is based on the authors' professional experience with Avon Products' Women of Enterprise Awards, given each year to outstanding women entrepreneurs. The authors offer a specific plan to help you gain control over your life and include business tips and quizzes as well as beauty and lifestyle information. ($17.95 cloth)

SIDE-BY-SIDE STRATEGIES: How Two-Career Couples Can Thrive in the Nineties, by Jane Hershey Cuozzo and S. Diane Graham, describes how two-career couples can learn the difference between competing with a spouse and becoming a supportive power partner. Published in hardcover as *Power Partners.* ($10.95 paper, $19.95 cloth)

DARE TO CONFRONT! How to Intervene When Someone You Care About Has an Alcohol or Drug Problem, by Bob Wright and Deborah George Wright, shows the reader how to use the step-by-step methods of professional interventionists to motivate drug-dependent people to accept the help they need. ($17.95 cloth)

WORK WITH ME! How to Make the Most of Office Support Staff, by Betsy Lazary, shows how to find, train, and nurture the "perfect" assistant and how best to utilize your support staff professionals. ($9.95 paper)

MANN FOR ALL SEASONS: Wit and Wisdom from The Washington Post's *Judy Mann,* by Judy Mann, shows the columnist at her best as she writes about women, families, and the politics of the women's revolution. ($9.95 paper, $19.95 cloth)

THE SOLUTION TO POLLUTION IN THE WORKPLACE, by Laurence Sombke, Terry M. Robertson and Elliot M. Kaplan, supplies employees with everything they need to know about cleaning up their workspace, including recycling, using energy efficiently, conserving water, and buying recycled products and nontoxic supplies. ($9.95 paper)

THE ENVIRONMENTAL GARDENER: The Solution to Pollution for Lawns and Gardens, by Laurence Sombke, focuses on what each of us can do to protect our endangered plant life. A practical sourcebook and shopping guide. ($8.95 paper)

THE LOYALTY FACTOR: Building Trust in Today's Workplace, by Carol Kinsey Goman, Ph.D., offers techniques for restoring commitment and loyalty in the workplace. ($9.95 paper)

DARE TO CHANGE YOUR JOB—AND YOUR LIFE, by Carole Kanchier, Ph.D., provides a look at career growth and development throughout the life cycle. ($10.95 paper)

MISS AMERICA: In Pursuit of the Crown, by Ann-Marie Bivans, is an authorized guidebook to the Pageant, containing eyewitness accounts, complete historical data, and a realistic look at the trials and triumphs of potential Miss Americas. ($27.50 cloth)

POSITIVELY OUTRAGEOUS SERVICE: New and Easy Ways to Win Customers for Life, by T. Scott Gross, identifies what the consumers of the nineties really want and how businesses can develop effective marketing strategies to answer those needs. ($14.95 paper)

BREATHING SPACE: Living and Working at a Comfortable Pace in a Sped-Up Society, by Jeff Davidson, helps readers to handle information and activity overload and gain greater control over their lives. ($10.95 paper)

TWENTYSOMETHING: Managing and Motivating Today's New Work Force, by Lawrence J. Bradford, Ph.D., and Claire Raines, M.A., examines the work orientation of the younger generation, offering managers in businesses of all kinds a practical guide to help them better understand and supervise their young employees. ($22.95 cloth)

BALANCING ACTS! Juggling Love, Work, Family and Recreation, by Susan Schiffer Stautberg and Marcia L. Worthing, provides strategies to achieve a balanced life by reordering priorities and setting realistic goals. ($12.95 paper)

THE LIVING HEART BRAND NAME SHOPPER'S GUIDE, by Michael E. DeBakey, M.D., Antonio M. Gotto, Jr., M.D., D.Phil., Lynne W. Scott, M.A., R.D./L.D., and John P. Foreyt, Ph.D., lists brand-name supermarket products that are low in fat, saturated fatty acids, and cholesterol. ($12.95 paper)

STEP FORWARD: Sexual Harassment in the Workplace, What You Need to Know, by Susan L. Webb, presents the facts for dealing with sexual harassment. ($9.95 paper)

REAL LIFE 101: The Graduate's Guide to Survival, by Susan Kleinman, supplies welcome advice to those facing "real life" for the first time, focusing on work, money, health, and dealing with freedom and responsibility. ($9.95 paper)

A TEEN'S GUIDE TO BUSINESS: The Secrets to a Successful Enterprise, by Linda Menzies, Oren S. Jenkins, and Rickell R. Fisher, provides solid information about starting your own business or working for one. ($7.95 paper)

THE OUTDOOR WOMAN: A Handbook to Adventure, by Patricia Hubbard and Stan Wass, details the lives of adventurous outdoor women and offers their ideas on how you can incorporate exciting outdoor experiences into your life. ($14.95 paper)

REAL BEAUTY . . . REAL WOMEN: A Workbook for Making the Best of Your Own Good Looks, by Kathleen Walas, International Beauty and Fashion Director of Avon Products, offers expert advice on beauty and fashion to women of all ages and ethnic backgrounds. ($19.50 paper)

MANAGING YOUR CHILD'S DIABETES, by Robert Wood Johnson IV, Sale Johnson, Casey Johnson, and Susan Kleinman, brings help to families trying to understand diabetes and control its effects. ($10.95 paper)

GLORIOUS ROOTS: Recipes for Healthy, Tasty Vegetables, by Laurence Sombke, celebrates the taste, texture, and versatility of root vegetables. Contains recipes for appetizers, soups, stews, and baked, boiled, and stir-fried dishes—even desserts. ($12.95 paper)

FLIGHT PLAN FOR LIVING: The Art of Self-Encouragement, by Patrick O'Dooley, is a life guide organized like a pilot's flight checklist, which ensures you'll be flying "clear on top" throughout your life. ($17.95 cloth)

HOW TO GET WHAT YOU WANT FROM ALMOST ANYBODY, by T. Scott Gross, shows how to get great service, negotiate better prices, and always get what you pay for. ($9.95 paper)

FINANCIAL SAVVY FOR WOMEN: A Money Book for Women of All Ages, by Dr. Judith Briles, divides a woman's monetary lifespan into six phases, discusses the specific areas to be addressed at each stage, and demonstrates how to create a sound lifelong money game plan. ($14.95 paper)

TEAMBUILT: Making Teamwork Work, by Mark Sanborn, teaches business how to improve productivity, without increasing resources or expenses, by building teamwork among employers. ($19.95 cloth)

THE BIG APPLE BUSINESS AND PLEASURE GUIDE: 501 Ways to Work Smarter, Play Harder, and Live Better in New York City, by Muriel Siebert and Susan Kleinman, offers visitors and New Yorkers alike advice on how to do business in the city as well as how to enjoy its attractions. ($9.95 paper)